SHASTRA ON THE DOOR TO UNDERSTANDING the hundred dharmas

by Vasubandhu Bodhisattva
with commentary of
Tripitaka Master Hua

Translated into English by
Dharma Realm Buddhist University
International Institute For The
Translation of Buddhist Texts

Talmage, California

1983

SHASTRA ON THE DOOR TO UNDERSTANDING THE HUNDRED DHARMAS

Translated into English by
THE BUDDHIST TEXT TRANSLATION SOCIETY:

Primary Translation: Bhikshuni Heng Hsien
                       Bhikshuni Heng Liang
Review of Translation: Bhikshuni Heng Ch'ih
Editing of Translation: Bhikshuni Heng Tao
Certification
    of Translation: Venerable Master Hua
                       & Bhikshuni Heng Ch'ih
                       & Bhikshuni Heng Tao

Printed in the United States of America
  First Printing: 1983, for Buddha's Birthday
For information, contact these centers:

Gold Mountain Monastery, 1731 15th Street, San
Francisco, California, 94103 tel. (415) 626-4204
                                   (415) 861-9672
Gold Wheel Monastery, 1728 West Sixth Street,
Los Angeles, California 90017 tel. (213) 483-7497

For information and book sales, contact:

Dharma Realm Buddhist University, Buddhist Text
Translation Society, City of Ten Thousand Buddhas,
Box 217, Talmage, Ca 95481   tel. (707) 642-0939

ISBN 0-88139-003-8

Acknowledgments:
    cover calligraphy: Bhikshuni Heng Liang
    typography and layout: Bhikshuni Heng Liang
                            Upasika Bina Teng
    index: Bhikshuni Heng Ch'ih
    proofreading: Bhikshuni Heng Chia
                    Upasika Susan Rounds
                    Upasika Marion Robertson
                    Upasika Barbara Waugh
    Chinese calligraphy: Bhikshuni Heng Duan

南無本師釋迦牟尼佛

Namo Shakyamuni Buddha

Buddhist Text Translation Society
Eight Regulations

A translator must free himself or herself from the motives of personal fame and reputation.

A translator must cultivate an attitude free from arrogance and conceit.

A translator must refrain from aggrandizing himself or herself and denigrating others.

A translator must not establish himself or herself as the standard of correctness and suppress the work of others with his or her faultfinding.

A translator must take the Buddha-mind as his or her own mind.

A translator must use the wisdom of the Selective Dharma Eye to determine true principles.

A translator must request the Elder Virtuous Ones of the ten directions to certify his or her translations.

A translator must endeavor to propagate the teachings by printing sutras, shastra texts, and vinaya texts when the translations are certified as being correct.

VENERABLE TRIPITAKA MASTER HSÜAN HUA

Verse Upon Opening A Sutra

The unsurpassed, deep, profound,
Subtle and wonderful Dharma,

In hundreds of millions of kalpas
Is difficult to encounter.

I now see and hear it,
Receive it and maintain it,

And I vow to understand the Thus Come One's
True and actual meaning.

TABLE OF CONTENTS

TABLE OF TRILINGUAL LISTS
(English, Chinese, Sanskrit)

SHASTRA
ON THE DOOR TO
UNDERSTANDING

the

hundred
dharmas

大乘百法名門論

天親菩薩造

三藏法師玄奘譯

如世尊言。一切法無我。何等一切法。云何爲無我。一切法者。略有五種。一者心法。二者心所有法。三者色法。四者心不相應行法。五者無爲法。一切最勝故。與此相應故。二所現影故。三位差別故。四所顯示故。如是次第。

第一心法。略有八種。一眼識。二耳識。三鼻識。四舌識。五身識。六意識。七末那識。八阿賴耶識。

第二心所有法。略有五十一種，分爲六位。一遍行有五。二別境有五。三

善有十一。四根本煩惱有六。五隨煩惱有二十。六不定有四。

一遍行五者。一作意。二觸。三受。四想。五思。

二別境五者。一欲。二勝解。三念。四三摩地。五慧。

三善十一者。一信。二精進。三慚。四愧。五無貪。六無瞋。七無癡。

八輕安。九不放逸。十行捨。十一不害。

四煩惱六者。一貪。二瞋。三癡。四慢。五疑。六不正見。五隨煩惱

二十者。一忿。二恨。三惱。四覆。五誑。六諂。七憍。八害。九嫉。十

慳。十一無慚。十二無愧。十三不信。十四懈怠。十五放逸。十六昏沉。

十七掉舉。十八失念。十九不正知。二十散亂。

六不定四者。一睡眠。二惡作。三尋。四伺。

第三色法。略有十一種。一眼。二耳。三鼻。四舌。五身。六色。七聲。

x

八香。九味。十觸。十一法處所攝色。

第四心不相應行法。略有二十四種。

一得。二命根。三眾同分。四異生性。五無想定。六滅盡定。七無想報。八名身。九句身。十文身。十一生。十二住。十三老。十四無常。十五流轉。十六定異。十七相應。十八勢速。十九次第。二十時。二十一方。二十二數。二十三和合性。二十四不和合性。

第五無為法者。略有六種。一虛空無為。二擇滅無為。三非擇滅無為。四不動滅無為。五想受滅無為。六真如無為。

言無我者。略有二種。一補特伽羅無我。二法無我。

SHASTRA ON THE DOOR TO
UNDERSTANDING THE HUNDRED DHARMAS

Composed by Vasubandhu
Bodhisattva
Translated by Tripitaka
Master Hsuan Tsang of
the T'ang Dynasty

As the World Honored One has said, "All dharmas have no self." What are all dharmas, and what is meant by having no self? All dharmas may be generally grouped into five categories:

ONE, MIND DHARMAS (*citta-dharmah*)

TWO, DHARMAS INTERACTIVE WITH THE MIND.
(*chaitasika-dharmah*)

THREE, FORM DHARMAS (*rupa-dharmah*)

FOUR, DHARMAS NOT INTERACTIVE WITH THE MIND
(*citta-viprayukta-samskara-dharmah*)

FIVE, UNCONDITIONED DHARMAS (*asamskrita-dharmah*)

They are in this sequence because the first are supreme, the second interact with the first, the third are the shadows manifest by the previous two, the fourth are the positions in which the previous three are not found, and the last are revealed by the previous four.

The first, MIND DHARMAS, include in general eight:

I. THE EYE CONSCIOUSNESS (*cakshur-vijnana*)
II. THE EAR CONSCIOUSNESS (*shrotra-vijnana*)
III. THE NOSE CONSCIOUSNESS (*ghrana-vijnana*)
IV. THE TONGUE CONSCIOUSNESS (*jihva-vijnana*)
V. THE BODY CONSCIOUSNESS (*kaya-vijnana*)

VI. THE MIND CONSCIOUSNESS (*mano-vijnana*)

VII. THE MANAS CONSCIOUSNESS (*manas-vijnana*)

VIII. THE ALAYA CONSCIOUSNESS (*alaya-vijnana*)

The second, DHARMAS INTERACTIVE WITH THE MIND, include, in general, fifty-one. They are divided into six categories:

I. THE FIVE UNIVERSALLY INTERACTIVE (*sarvatraga*)

II. THE FIVE PARTICULAR STATES (*viniyata*)

III. THE ELEVEN WHOLESOME (*kushala*)

IV. THE SIX FUNDAMENTAL AFFLICTIONS (*klesha*)

V. THE TWENTY DERIVATIVE AFFLICTIONS (*upaklesha*)

VI. THE FOUR UNFIXED (*aniyata*)

I. THE FIVE UNIVERSALLY INTERACTIVE are:

    1. ATTENTION (*manaskara*)

    2. CONTACT (*sparsha*)

    3. FEELING (*vedana*)

    4. CONCEPTUALIZATION (*samjna*)

    5. DELIBERATION (*cetana*)

II. THE FIVE PARTICULAR STATES are:

    1. DESIRE (*chanda*)

    2. RESOLUTION (*adhimoksha*)

    3. RECOLLECTION (*smriti*)

    4. CONCENTRATION (*samadhi*)

    5. JUDGMENT (*prajna*)

III. THE ELEVEN WHOLESOME DHARMAS are:
1. FAITH (*shraddha*)
2. VIGOR (*virya*)
3. SHAME (*hri*)
4. REMORSE (*apatrapya*)
5. ABSENCE OF GREED (*alobha*)
6. ABSENCE OF ANGER (*advesha*)
7. ABSENCE OF STUPIDITY (*amoha*)
8. LIGHT EASE (*prashrabdhi*)
9. NON-LAXNESS (*apramada*)
10. RENUNCIATION (*upeksha*)
11. NON-HARMING (*ahimsa*)

IV. THE SIX FUNDAMENTAL AFFLICTIONS are:
1. GREED (*raga*)
2. ANGER (*pratigha*)
3. STUPIDITY (*moha*)
4. ARROGANCE (*mana*)
5. DOUBT (*vicikitsa*)
6. IMPROPER VIEWS (*drishti*)

V. THE TWENTY DERIVATIVE AFFLICTIONS are:
(A. *Ten Minor Grade Afflictions*)
1. WRATH (*krodha*)
2. HATRED (*upanaha*)
3. RAGE (*pradasa*)
4. COVERING (*mraksha*)
5. DECEIT (*maya*)
6. FLATTERY (*shathya*)
7. CONCEIT (*mada*)
8. HARMING (*vihimsa*)
9. JEALOUSY (*irshya*)
10. STINGINESS (*matsarya*)

(B. *The Two Intermediate-Grade Afflictions*)

11. LACK OF SHAME (*ahrikya*)
12. LACK OF REMORSE (*anapatrapya*)

(C. *The Eight Major-Grade Afflictions*)

13. LACK OF FAITH (*ashraddhya*)
14. LAZINESS (*kausidya*)
15. LAXNESS (*pramada*)
16. TORPOR (*styana*)
17. RESTLESSNESS (*auddhatya*)
18. DISTRACTION (*mushitasmriti*)
19. IMPROPER KNOWLEDGE (*asamprajanya*)
20. SCATTEREDNESS (*vikshepa*)

VI. THE FOUR UNFIXED are:
1. SLEEP (*middha*)
2. REGRET (*kaukritya*)
3. EXAMINATION (*vitarka*)
4. INVESTIGATION (*vicara*)

The third is the FORM DHARMAS. In general, there are eleven kinds:

I. EYES (*cakshus*)
II. EARS (*shrotra*)
III. NOSE (*ghrana*)
IV. TONGUE (*jihva*)
V. BODY (*kaya*)
VI. FORMS (*rupa*)
VII. SOUNDS (*shabda*)
VIII. SMELLS (*gandha*)
IX. FLAVORS (*rasa*)
X. OBJECTS OF TOUCH (*sprashtavya*)
XI. DHARMAS PERTAINING TO FORM (*dharmayatanikani rupani*)

The fourth is the DHARMAS NOT INTERACTIVE WITH THE MIND. In general, there are twenty-four:

I. ATTAINMENT (AQUISITION) (prapti)
II. LIFE-FACULTY (jivitendriya)
III. GENERIC SIMILARITY (nikaya-sabhaga)
IV. DISSIMILARITY (visabhaga)
V. THE NO-THOUGHT SAMADHI (asamjnisamapatti)
VI. THE SAMADHI OF EXTINCTION (nirodha-samapatti)
VII. THE REWARD OF NO THOUGHT (asamjnika)
VIII. BODIES OF NOUNS (namakaya)
IX. BODIES OF SENTENCES (padakaya)
X. BODIES OF PHONEMES (vyanjanakaya)
XI. BIRTH (jati)
XII. DWELLING (sthiti)
XIII. AGING (jara)
XIV. IMPERMANENCE (anityata)
XV. REVOLUTION (pravritti)
XVI. DISTINCTION (pratiniyama)
XVII. INTERACTION (yoga)
XVIII. SPEED (java)
XIX. SEQUENCE (anukrama)
XX. TIME (kala)
XXI. DIRECTION (desha)
XXII. NUMERATION (samkhya)
XXIII. COMBINATION (samagri)
XXIV. DISCONTINUITY (anyathatva)

The fifth is the UNCONDITIONED DHARMAS, of which there are, in general, six:

I. UNCONDITIONED EMPTY SPACE (akasha)
II. UNCONDITIONED EXTINCTION WHICH IS ATTAINED BY SELECTION (pratisamkhyanirodha)

What is meant by there being no self? There are, in general, Two Kinds of Non-Self: 1. The Non-self of Pudgala, and 2. the Non-self of Dharmas.

INTRODUCTION

The Dharma spoken by the Buddha constitutes the Sutras, the precepts which the Buddha established make up the Vinaya, and the writings of the Patriarchs are called the Shastras. Sutras reveal the study of samadhi, Vinaya texts disclose the study of precepts, and Shastras discuss the study of wisdom. You could say this is the first time since the founding of the Buddhist Lecture Hall here in San Francisco that a Shastra is being thoroughly explained. Although we have had classes on Shastras before, the explanations have been quite simple. This explanation will go into more depth. A lecture series like this is very rare in the West, which is why when people in the West wish to learn to understand Shastras there is almost no opportunity to do so. But if you don't understand the Shastras, you won't be able to cultivate. If you can't cultivate, you won't become a Buddha. And if you don't become a Buddha, you will revolve forever on the wheel of rebirth, being born then dying, and after dying being reborn. When born, you are completely muddled and don't know what happened, and at the time of death you are just about to understand but time won't wait for you. You die just as muddled, and much as you would like to understand, there's no more time. The reason you don't understand is that you have not investigated THE SHASTRA ON THE DOOR TO UNDERSTANDING THE HUNDRED DHARMAS, and so you're born muddled and die confused over and over again as you turn in the six paths of the revolving wheel. So now we are lecturing this Shastra.

Someone may ask, "What is THE SHASTRA ON THE DOOR TO UNDERSTANDING THE HUNDRED DHARMAS? Not only have I never seen it, I've never even heard of it before."

That's good. You speak very honestly. When you know you say you know, and when you don't know you say you don't. That means you can still be taught. The trouble is that many people tend to say they know something when they do not in fact know it. If one doesn't know something but says one does, in an attempt to fool people, one is

actually only fooling oneself. Someone who claims
to know what he doesn't know and denies knowing
what he does know is the stupidest kind of person.
To pretend to know what one does not in fact know
is the dumbest thing one can do. An example would
be if you have never heard of THE SHASTRA ON THE DOOR
TO UNDERSTANDING THE HUNDRED DHARMAS, but when someone
asks you if you're familiar with it you reply, "Oh,
I know that one." Then when asked what the Shastra
discusses you say, "Oh, I've forgotten." That's
a clear-cut case of saying you know what you do
not in fact know, saying you have mastered what you
haven't mastered, saying you understand what you
do not understand, and claiming to be perfectly
clear about what is not at all clear to you. That
is the stupidest thing a person can do, and it
leads to rebirth as a pig. People who get reborn
as pigs were great pretenders in their former lives
and acted as though they knew absolutely everything.
That's why I feel such pity for pigs when I encounter them. I tell them, "You are lamentable. You
just wouldn't listen to instructions in the least.
You didn't rely upon the Dharma to cultivate, and
so you've fallen into the bodies of pigs."

　　There aren't just one hundred dharmas; there
are 660 dharmas. But actually there aren't just
660 dharmas; there are really 84,000 dharmas. The
Buddha set forth 84,000 Dharma doors, and every
door is a path to accomplishing Buddhahood. Later
on, because living beings' basic natures were too
stupid, 84,000 Dharma doors became too many. Therefore, Maitreya Bodhisattva very compassionately
composed the *Yogacharyabhumi Shastra* (T. 1579), which
consolidated the 84,000 Dharma doors into 660
dharmas. But 660 dharmas were still quite a few,
and just to clearly remember their names took
several years of effort. Then Vasubandhu--"Heavenly
Relative"--Bodhisattva contemplated and saw that
people in the future whose natures were suited to
the Great Vehicle would prefer abbreviation. So
he selected the one hundred most important leading
dharmas from the *Yogacharyabhumi Shastra's* 660 dharmas
and condensed them into THE SHASTRA ON THE DOOR TO UN-
DERSTANDING THE HUNDRED DHARMAS. That way all people in
the world with dispositions suited to the Great
Vehicle could easily remember and understand its
dharmas and no longer have to spend several years

just to remember their names. The most dense person could memorize these Dharma doors in an hour, and the smartest person could understand all one hundred dharmas in as little as ten minutes' time. Wouldn't you say that was fast? If you understand these hundred dharmas, you can use them to enter the door of the Buddhadharma. That's why it's called the "Door to Understanding," for if you understand these hundred dharmas, you can enter the door of the Buddhadharma.

Before explaining THE SHASTRA ON THE DOOR TO UNDERSTANDING THE HUNDRED DHARMAS, I would first like to level a criticism. From what I have seen and heard of people in the West who explain the Buddhadharma, if you were to ask them what THE SHASTRA ON THE DOOR TO UNDERSTANDING THE HUNDRED DHARMAS is, what reply would they give? They would not say a word. Now, that would definitely not be as when Manjushri Bodhisattva asked Upasaka Vimalakirti what truth in the primary sense was, and Upasaka Vimalakirti did not say anything at all. His not speaking itself was truth in the primary sense. If he had spoken, truth in the primary sense would have vanished. So he really did express truth in the primary sense by his silence. But the hundred dharmas are not the same as truth in the primary sense. They must be spoken. If instead of speaking you close your mouth, close your eyes, and put on a big show of studying truth in the primary sense, you're wrong. That's because the very fact that there are one hundred kinds of dharmas means they have to be expressed. Without speaking there is no way to represent those hundred dharmas. But the reason the Western "speakers of Dharma" pull the silent act is that they simply do not understand them. Not to speak of one hundred, they couldn't even expound a single dharma. Since they can't explain even one, they have nothing to say. All they can do is go into some kind of tight-lipped, mystic-eyed trance. Wouldn't you say that was sad? But although there is not a single dharma they understand or speak, still they go outside the hundred dharmas to talk about "Dharma" left and right, up and down. And people who don't understand the Buddhadharma say, "That person can really speak Dharma." But as soon as people who already understand the Buddhadharma hear him, they say, "What is that nonsense all about? He's just singing a song."

This is as when a counterfeiter takes his
counterfeit money to the countryside and passes it
off to people who can't tell it's not real. But
later at the mint they can see right away that the
hallmarks and serial numbers are completely wrong
and that the money is phony. It's proved false
when compared to the true. In the same way, it
may be "Dharma" spoken, but you have to have the
Dharma-selecting Eye to tell Dharma from non-Dharma
and to distinguish which are defiled and which are
pure dharmas, which are wholesome and which are
unwholesome dharmas, which are deviant and which
are proper dharmas. If you know, then you have
the Dharma-selecting Eye. It should not be that
if someone speaks "Dharma" in a booming voice, or
sings it like a wailing chant, you become so confused you couldn't sleep even if you wanted to.
Wouldn't you say that was pathetic?!

EXPLANATION OF THE TITLE

Well, I can't sing, so I'll talk a bit. The
Hundred Dharmas are derived like this: one becomes
ten and ten become one hundred. The Hundred Dharmas divide into Form Dharmas, Mind Dharmas, Dharmas
Interactive with the Mind, Dharmas Not Interactive
with the Mind and Unconditioned Dharmas.
THE HUNDRED DHARMAS divide into:

    11 kinds of form dharmas
     8 kinds of mind dharmas
    51 dharmas interactive
         with the mind
    24 dharmas not interactive
         with the mind
     6 unconditioned dharmas.

Each of these kinds in each of these categories
will be explained in the Shastra proper. They
won't be explained in detail now while we are explaining the title. If we explained them thoroughly
right now, there would be nothing to discuss when
we got to the Shastra itself. So now the kinds
and numbers of each are mentioned, and if you understand all about them from that, then you don't
have to come back to listen any more. But if you
don't understand what they are all about yet, then
you'll have to return to hear more about them. People will go home wondering, "What did he mean by
eleven kinds of form dharmas, eight kinds of mind
dharmas? That Dharma Master just brought up their
names but he didn't tell us anything about them.
I really don't want to go back and listen again,
but then, there will always remain in my mind this
matter that I never got clear about. I'm going to
have to go listen." So now you see why, when in-
troducing the title, we don't go into detail.
That's logical enough, wouldn't you say?
Someone who lectures the Sutras and Shastras
has to have a pattern to his talks. He has to have
good timing. Then there will be no way for those
seriously interested in hearing the Shastra to fail
to come and listen. If, of course, the person has
the attitude, "I'm not the least bit interested in
learning what you mean by a hundred dharmas, or a
thousand dharmas or a million dharmas. I don't

even care about a single dharma," then there's
nothing to be said. But if you are someone who
would like to understand the Buddhadharma, then
you are definitely going to want to come and listen.

DOOR TO UNDERSTANDING means, in the first place,
not being confused, not being muddled, and not being stupid. It means clarity, clarity about the
path of these hundred Dharma doors which enable
one to cultivate.

SHASTRA is a Sanskrit word which means discussion, discourse. We can use that interpretation
here and say that this explanation of the Shastra
is also a discussion, and that anyone who doesn't
agree with the way I explain it can bring up his
or her own theories and we will discuss them. That
means, if you have questions, I can answer you. A
discourse refers to an expression of one's principles. You say what yours are and I say what
mine are and then we can discuss them and investigate the Dharma. However, the Dharma I speak is
not my Dharma. What I express is the Buddhadharma.
If anyone thinks that I am speaking incorrectly,
all you have to do is bring up your reasons and
we'll investigate them. I can meet any of your
objections. You can come at me with objections and
I can answer them all. It includes all the people
in the entire world, no matter what their nation-
ality. Anyone at all can bring up his or her principles and we will hold a huge symposium. I can
answer any question put by any person throughout
the ten directions.

"Aha!"   you wonder. "How can people come
from the ten directions? I can see them coming
from four directions or eight directions, but from
ten?" Well, now we have airplanes, so suppose
someone lands right here in a helicopter--he's
come from the upper direction, right? And someone
out of a submarine from the sea is equivalent to
coming out of the earth, right? So I say again,
anyone throughout the ten directions can ask any
question they want and we will hold a large symposium to discuss the Buddhadharma. It makes no
difference what religion they subscribe to--Bud-
dhism or any other. If they have a question, they
can come and ask it. If they have some difficulty,
I will use my sword of wisdom to slice right through
it for them. I'll slice out their tongues, if

need be. Then they won't be able to say anything
more. You should be clear about this, however.
I will slice out their tongues of stupidity, leaving their tongues of wisdom. I'll remove their
tongues of stupidity and replace them with tongues
of wisdom. I'm capable of making tongue transplants as well as brain transplants. If their
brains are unclear, I can give them a new set.

Now we'll discuss the word "Shastra." You'll
remember I said a bit ago that the Hundred Dharmas
must be expressed. Why? If they weren't expressed
there would be no Shastra. Shastras are discussions. First of all, they tell what is right and
what is wrong. Right is right and wrong is definitely wrong. One must not take what is right as
wrong, nor should one take what is wrong as right.
So we discuss things and in this way come to understand them clearly. For people who leave the
home life, cultivation is right and failing to cultivate is wrong.

The second thing which Shastras discuss is
what is deviant and what is proper. What is deviant
is definitely deviant and what is proper is decidedly proper. You must not take what is deviant
and consider it to be proper, nor take what is
proper and consider it to be deviant. That's
another reason why there must be discussions.

The third reason for discussions is to distinguish good and evil. Good is good and evil is
evil. You cannot regard what is good as being
evil, nor regard what is evil as being good.

The fourth function of Shastras is to discuss
cause and effect. A cause is decidedly a cause
and an effect is definitely an effect. You can't
call a cause an effect, nor an effect a cause.
You must make your discriminations clearly.

The fifth aspect of Shastras is to clarify
defilement and purity. Defilement is defilement
and purity is purity. You must not take defilement to be purity or purity to be defilement. You
must not be upside down. So what Shastras do is
discriminate these clearly.

However, it is true that right can turn into
wrong, and that wrong can become right. If you

get rid of what's wrong, then you are right. If
you dispense with what is right, you are wrong.
The other four meanings also contain this qualifi-
cation.
     To sum up, Shastras are discussions of,

>   1. right and wrong
>   2. deviant and proper
>   3. good and evil
>   4. cause and effect
>   5. defilement and purity

They have those five functions and are thus able
to delineate dharmas quite precisely. We can also
say, however, that the right is not apart from the
wrong and vice-versa. What is right is wrong; what
is wrong is right. What is good is just evil and
what is evil is just good. What is deviant is itself proper; what is proper is itself deviant.
What is cause is just effect; what is effect is
just cause. What is defilement is just purity;
what is purity is just defilement. So now you see
that when it comes to discussions, you can discuss
things any way you want. It's just to be feared
you don't have anything to discuss. You say right
is wrong and wrong is right? Well, let's see how
you explain that. That's the way questions are
investigated. "How is it done?" you ask. If you
don't know, then you have to study. After you
study you'll know it yourself. That's the wonder
of it. If you know a little Buddhadharma, you
can't recognize that there's a lot of it. But if
you know a lot of it, you can't say there's only
a little.
     This has been a general explanation of the
title: THE SHASTRA ON THE DOOR TO UNDERSTANDING THE
HUNDRED DHARMAS. Discussion finished!

THE AUTHOR

Text:

Composed by Vasubandhu Bodhisattva.

Commentary:

This Shastra was composed by Vasubandhu Bodhisattva, whose given name translates as "Heavenly Relative" and also as "The Lord's Relative." Some say that he was the younger brother of Lord God. There's really no need to try and research this; people just take it on faith. Vasubandhu Bodhisattva had two brothers. Vasubandhu was their family name. His elder brother's name was Asanga, which translates as "unattached". "Heavenly Relative" was the second-born and the youngest of the three was named Virincivatsa. "Virinci" was their mother's name and "vatsa" is the Sanskrit word which means "son of". So he was known as "the son of Virinci". But this brother is too young to come into our present discussion other than to be introduced to you. All three of these brothers were extremely intelligent. They lived during the period of time about nine hundred years after the Buddha entered Nirvana. However, although they were intelligent, still, each had his prejudiced views in the beginning. Later on they gave up their prejudices.

To begin with, the eldest brother wanted to be "unattached," and although he had no attachments, he preferred the Great Vehicle Buddhadharma. Heavenly Relative was attached to Small Vehicle Buddhadharma. He felt that it was the true Buddhadharma, and he not only studied it but aided those involved in Small Vehicle Buddhism in berating and slandering the Great Vehicle.

Even though his older brother studied Great Vehicle Buddhism, Heavenly Relative still said it wasn't true--that the Buddha did not actually speak the *Dharma Flower Sutra*, the *Shurangama Sutra*, and the *Flower Adornment Sutra*. He, in fact, became a specialist in undermining Great Vehicle Dharma. So here we have two brothers--the elder of whom studied Great Vehicle Dharma but did not criticize the

Small Vehicle at all, while the younger brother who studied the Small Vehicle criticized and tried to destroy the Great Vehicle. So they didn't actually fight, because the contention was only on the side of Heavenly Relative. The whole reason that the Great Vehicle is called by that name is because Great Vehicle Buddhadharma can even include within it that which is incorrect. But the Small Vehicle cannot include what is not correct within it. That's why it is so small. The Great Vehicle can include what is correct and what is incorrect. So, no matter how many offenses his younger brother had, Asanga did not hold them against him and even wanted to save him.

What method did Asanga use to save Heavenly Relative? He wrote his younger brother saying, "Although we do not study the same teachings, still, our relationship as brothers is a fact. We are close relatives for sure and we both acknowledge this true relationship which exists between us. Now, I know that I am going to die pretty soon and I'd like to see you. This is especially so because I would like your help in doing something, and I believe that you'll fulfill my wish in spite of everything. If you don't do this for me, then when I die, I won't be able to close my eyes." Notice that he didn't say he *was* dying, but said, "...when I die," leaving the time unfixed.

How could a younger brother not respond to such a sincere letter? Even though they studied two different teachings, Heavenly Relative decided he should go visit his brother Asanga. When he got there he asked what it was his elder brother wished him to do, so that Asanga would be able to close his eyes when he died. Asanga said, "I would like you to help me recite the *Dharma Flower Sutra*, the *Shurangama Sutra*, and the *Flower Adornment Sutra*. I would like you to read each one of them through for me." That was the method he chose, because he knew his younger brother was extremely intelligent and never forgot anything he read.

Thereupon Heavenly Relative, in order to fulfill his elder brother's last wish, proceeded to do something which he really didn't want to do. He read those Sutras aloud for his brother Asanga. When he'd finished reading the *Dharma Flower Sutra*, the *Shurangama Sutra*, and the *Avatamsaka Sutra* --those three Great Vehicle Sutras--he knew that he'd been

Vasubandhu Bodhisattva

completely wrong in the past for criticizing and
berating the Great Vehicle Buddhadharma and slandering the Great Vehicle Sutras. He had gone about
saying that those Sutras were inauthentic. He now
knew how mistaken he'd been and he felt tremendous
regret. He became a bit frantic thinking, "What
shall I do? I've spent so much time and energy in
slandering the Great Vehicle Buddhadharma. It's
for sure those offenses will cause me to fall into
the hells. There's no question about it. What a
despicable tongue I have!" Whereupon he grabbed
a knife and was bent upon cutting out his own
tongue.

Why did I say earlier that I would cut out
people's tongues--their dumb tongues, their dull-
witted tongues, their stupid tongues? It's just
because Heavenly Relative Bodhisattva himself
wanted to slice out his own tongue. He wanted to
get rid of his stupid tongue. Anyway, you can
imagine the tenseness of the situation. Heavenly
Relative had his tongue pulled out and the knife
poised over it, ready to lay the blow. It was no
joking matter. He was really going to do it. At
that point his elder brother Unattached said sooth-
ingly, "Second brother, what are you doing? How
about telling me what you're up to?"

Heavenly Relative said, "My offenses are too
great. I've been continually slandering the Great
Vehicle Buddhadharma. Now upon reading those three
Sutras, I know that the doctrines of the Great
Vehicle are incomparably wonderful. My slander of
the Great Vehicle is going to put me in the 'Hell
of Pulling Out Tongues' is it not? So I'll just
cut out my own tongue right now while I'm still
alive. What do you think of this idea?" He asked
his elder brother's advice.

Unattached replied, "Don't be so dumb. You
can exchange your tongue."

"What do you mean? How?"asked the distraught
Heavenly Relative.

"Before,you used your tongue to slander; now,
you can use it to praise Great Vehicle Sutras. All
you have to do is change your way of talking.
That's a much more positive way of going about it.
There's no need to cut your tongue out."

Hearing that, Heavenly Relative thought, "He's
right. If I cut out my tongue, of what use will
that be to Great Vehicle Buddhism? I'll change
and praise Great Vehicle Buddhism with it, instead."

Thinking it through in this way, Heavenly
Relative's natural wisdom appeared and he then composed THE SHASTRA ON THE DOOR TO UNDERSTANDING THE HUNDRED
DHARMAS. So he was a person who changed his faults.
He had courageous spirit and valiantly changed what
was wrong with him. When he said he was going to
change, he actually did it. And after that, all
the books he wrote were in praise of the Great Vehicle. He destroyed all the books he'd previously
written, and the Shastras he wrote in praise of the
Great Vehicle circulated all over the world.
    BODHISATTVA (Bodhi = "enlighten ent" + Sattva
= "being": "sentient being")is a Sanskrit word
which translates in two ways:
    1. Enlightener of Sentient Beings. The Bo-
dhisattva takes the enlightenment that he has tes-
tified to, the wisdom that he has opened, and uses
that enlightened wisdom to enlighten all other
beings with sentience.
    2. An Enlightened Sentient Being. The Bodhi-
sattva is also a sentient being, but he is one who
has become enlightened.
    Put together, these two meanings show that a
Bodhisattva is an enlightened sentient being who
enlightens other sentient beings. That is the
meaning of "Bodhisattva".
    "Bodhisattva" is a pretty good name to have,
so lots of people want to give themselves that
title. They want to get others to call them by
that name. In China,   left-home people call
each other "Bodhisattva". But "Bodhisattva" is a
title which someone else should bestow upon one.
It's not that people decide they should be called
that and give themselves that name. On the other
hand, there was Great Master T'ai Shü who said,
"All people should call me 'Bodhisattva' instead
of 'Bhikshu'. Why? It's because I've already become
a Bhikshu, but not yet become a Buddha. That's because one takes the Bhikshu and the Bodhisattva
Precepts at full ordination. I've received the
Bodhisattva Precepts so you should all call me
'Bodhisattva'. But I haven't become a Buddha yet,
so don't call me a 'Buddha'." In that case, he
was just joking. In fact, Great Master T'ai Shü
was a Bodhisattva, so whether or not anyone called
him that made absolutely no difference. It's just
for that reason he was able to joke in that way.

He was chiding dim-witted living beings when he
said, "You should all call me 'Bodhisattva,'" just
as was the Living Buddha of Gold Mountain when he
announced that everyone should call him a living
Buddha. Both those comments were made in the same
spirit.

But in this case, was it that Heavenly Relative, who COMPOSED this Shastra, signed his name,
"Heavenly Relative Bodhisattva"? No. He just
signed his name to the Shastra without adding any
titles. It was devoted scholars later on who, out
of reverence for him, added that title to his name.
It wasn't like now when people who get Ph.D.'s have
that printed on their calling cards and go about
advertising their status. I regularly say to such
people--with no malice intended--"What's so great
about a Ph.D., anyway? You've got a Ph.D. So
what?" Ph.D....Cats could be Ph.D.s; dogs could,
too. Why? Because it has no value. The point is
that if you have what it takes, you don't need to
praise yourself. It's better for others to do the
praising. The same applies to left-home people who
add the title "Dharma Master" to their names when
printing their cards or giving their names, because
they like the sound of the title. But that title
is not something one gives oneself. Therefore,
I'm sure that Heavenly Relative Bodhisattva did
not add a title to his name. Everyone should look
into this. Don't become infatuated with name and
fame. It's better to call yourself a dead person
or a corpse. Pick a name nobody else wants and
then no one will fight you for it. I believe that's
a better solution. It's said:

> The superior person goes without a name.
> The inferior person is fond of titles.

Which you want to be is up to you.

TRANSLATOR

Text:

Translated by Tripitaka Master Hsuan Tsang of the T'ang Dynasty.

Commentary:

Now we will discuss the translator. The Shastra was composed in Sanskrit--the language of India --so it had to be translated in order to be studied by those of other countries. If it hadn't been translated, then only Indian people would have been able to understand it, and people of other countries would not have had a chance to learn from it. The person who translated this Sutra, therefore, has a lot of merit and virtue. If because of studying this Shastra we are able to understand all dharmas and rely upon dharmas to cultivate, we have the translator to thank in part. So we should first know who the translator was and what contributions he made within Buddhism.

He was OF THE T'ANG DYNASTY. This Bhikshu's contributions to Buddhism have been exceptionally great. It can be said that from ancient times to the present, there has never been anyone who can compare to this Dharma Master in his achievements. His worldly surname was Ch'a. His father was an official, but a poor one. Why did he end up a poor official? It was because he didn't take bribes. He wasn't after the citizens' money nor that of the government. He wasn't like people of these days who hold office and always feel they are earning too little money so that on top of their government salary they force the citizens to give them their hard-earned money as well. Dharma Master Hsuan Tsang's father didn't want money. He remained a poor official all his life. Even though he was poor, he had a virtuous nature and because of that he had two sons who left the home-life, lectured Sutras, and were adept cultivators of the Way.

Dharma Master Hsuan Tsang left the home-life at the age of thirteen and commenced his study of the Buddhadharma. During those early years of

study, if there was a Dharma Master lecturing a
Buddhist text, no matter who the Dharma Master was
or how far away the lecture was being held, he was
sure to go to listen, whether it was a Sutra lecture, a Shastra lecture, or a Vinaya lecture. He
went to listen to them all. Wind and rain couldn't
keep him away from lectures on the Tripitaka, to
the point that he even forgot to be hungry. He
just ate the Dharma, taking the Buddhadharma as his
food and drink. He did this for five years and
then took the Complete Precepts.

However, the principles lectured by the Dharma
Masters he heard were all different. They all explained the same Sutras in very different ways--
each with his own interpretation. And there was
a big difference between the lectures of those with
wisdom and those without wisdom. But Dharma Master
Hsuan Tsang had not yet really opened enlightenment
and he didn't have the Selective Dharma Eye, so
how could he know whose lectures to rely on? At
that time he vowed to go to India, saying,

> The Buddhadharma has been transmitted
> from India, and so there is certainly true
> and genuine Buddhadharma to be found in
> India.

Thereupon, he wrote a request for permission to go
to India to seek the Dharma and presented it to the
Emperor. The Emperor T'ai Tsung of T'ang did not
grant his wish, but Dharma Master Hsuan Tsang, who
had already vowed to go, said, "I would prefer to
disobey the Son of Heaven and have my head cut off
than not to go and seek the Dharma." So he returned to the monastery and began to practice
mountain-climbing. He piled chairs, tables, and
benches together to simulate a mountain and practiced jumping from one piece of furniture to the
next. This was his method of practicing mountain-
climbing. From morning 'til night he leaped from
table to chair. Probably there weren't any big
mountains where he lived, so he had to practice in
the temple. All the young, old and older novices
wondered what he was up to, jumping on furniture
all day long instead of reciting Sutras or cultivating. He didn't tell anyone that he was training
to climb the Himalayas, so most people thought he
was goofing off. Eventually he trained his body

Tripitaka Master Hsuan Tsang

so that it was very strong, and then when he was
physically able, he started his trip through
Siberia.

On the day of his departure, when the Emperor
T'ai Tsung learned he intended to go even without
Imperial consent, the Emperor asked him, "I haven't
given you permission and you still insist on going.
When will you be back?"

Dharma Master Hsuan Tsang replied, "Look at
this pine tree. The needles are pointing toward
the west. Wait until those needles turn around
and face east. That is the time when I will return." He didn't say how many years that would be.
So he set out. At that time there were no airplanes, steamboats, buses, or trains. There were
boats, but they were made of wood and not too
sturdy. Besides, since he didn't have Imperial
permission, he probably could not have gotten the
use of a boat anyway. So he traveled by land
through many countries, from the Siberian area of
the Russian border to India. He was gone for more
than a decade. When he reached India, he didn't
know the language at all. But bit-by-bit he studied Sanskrit and listened to many Dharma Masters
lecture the Buddhadharma. Some people say this
took him fourteen years. Others say it took nine-
teen. In general, he went through a great deal of
suffering and difficulty to study the Buddhadharma
and then when he'd completed his studies, he returned to China.

When his return was imminent, the needles on
the pine tree turned to the east. As soon as the
Emperor saw that the pine needles were indeed
pointing east, he knew that Dharma Master Hsuan
Tsang was coming back and he sent out a party of
officials to the western gate to welcome and es-
cort him back. When they reached the gate, there,
indeed, was Dharma Master Tsang returning.

Dharma Master Hsuan Tsang then concentrated
on translating the Sutras and other works that he
had brought back with him. He translated from
Sanskrit into Chinese.   At the time when he
was translating the *Great Prajna Sutra*, within that
one single year, the peach trees blossomed six
times. That was a sign of the auspiciousness of
the *Great Prajna Sutra* and its importance to all of
us. The fact that it was being translated moved
even the wood and plants to display their delight.

Dharma Master Tsang translated a great many Sutras. While in India, he bowed to the Buddha's Sharira and bones. He saw where the Buddha in a previous life had given up his eyes, and went to the place where the Buddha in a previous life had given up his head. He visited the place where the Buddha in a previous life had practiced the conduct of patience, and went to the place where the Buddha in a previous life had given up his life for the sake of a tiger. He also went to see the Bodhi tree under which the Buddha accomplished the Way. He went to all of those places celebrated in Buddhism. These pilgrimages are another indication of the extent of his true sincerity. While in India, whenever he met Dharma Masters, he never looked down on them, no matter how little they may have cultivated. He was extremely respectful. He wasn't the least bit arrogant or haughty. When he finished his studies, many Small Vehicle Dharma Masters and masters of externalist ways came to debate with him, but none were able to defeat him.

Dharma Master Hsuan Tsang is known as a TRIPITAKA MASTER (Tripitaka = "Three Stores, Three Baskets"). The Tripitaka includes the Sutra Store, the Shastra Store and the Vinaya Store. He was honored with this title because he understood all three Stores without any obstruction.

A Dharma Master is:

1. One who bestows the Dharma
   upon people.
2. One who takes the Dharma
   as his Master.

As to his name, HSUAN means "esoteric and wonderful". He was esoteric in the sense that none could really understand him. TSANG means "awe-inspiring". He was awe-inspiring in that he could do what others could not do. He was an outstanding person among his peers. His wisdom surpassed all those around him. He is the one who translated this SHASTRA ON THE DOOR TO UNDERSTANDING THE HUNDRED DHARMAS. Because the Dharma Master understood both Chinese and Sanskrit, he didn't make mistakes in his translations of the Sutras, and his translations of Shastras are also totally reliable.

The Three Cart Patriarch

At that time, Dharma Master Hsuan Tsang had eight hundred Bhikshus helping him translate the Sutras spoken by the Buddha. They were a group of extremely talented people. The most renowned among them was Dharma Master K'uei Chi. He was known as the "Three Cart Patriarch". Why was he called that? It's because prior to his leaving the home-life he presented some conditions to the Emperor. His consenting to the imperial edict he had received ordering him to leave the home-life was contingent upon being given three carts. He wanted these three carts to follow him wherever he went. One of these carts was to be filled with wine. Basically monks don't drink wine, but he considered himself special. Another cart was to carry fresh meat because he liked to eat it, and the third cart had to contain beautiful women. Now you see how he got his nickname. But you should be clear that the Three Cart Patriarch was not an ordinary person. For one thing, no ordinary person would dare present such conditions to the Emperor when he had been ordered to leave the home-life. In order to understand how special he was, we have to look into his previous life.

When Dharma Master Hsuan Tsang was on his way to India, he encountered an old cultivator way up in the mountains. The old cultivator had been meditating there for so long that the dust which had accumulated on his clothing was an inch or more thick. The birds had obviously made a seasonal thing of nesting in his hair. They built their nest, laid their eggs, and reared their young while he remained there in samadhi. It would be hard to say how many years he'd been sitting in that same spot unmoving. Anyway, Dharma Master Hsuan Tsang rang his bell to bring him out of samadhi. The old fellow came out of samadhi all right, but he couldn't move. He was as stiff as a board. But he was able to ask, "Why did you ring the bell and bring me out of meditation?"

Dharma Master Hsuan Tsang asked him, "Old cultivator, how long have you been sitting here in samadhi? What's the sense of never coming out of meditation?"

The old cultivator replied, "I'm waiting for the Red Yang Buddha to come into the world. Then

I'm going to help him propagate the Buddhadharma.
Dharma Master Hsuan Tsang said, "But the Red
Yang Buddha has come and gone already. He entered
the world and has already passed into Nirvana. You
sat here and didn't even know the Red Yang Buddhadharma was in the world."

"Well what time is it?" asked the cultivator,
and Dharma Master Hsuan Tsang related that he was
from the T'ang Dynasty. "That's all right," said
the cultivator. "If the Red Yang Buddha has come
and gone, I'll wait for the White Yang Buddha," and he
prepared to go back into samadhi.

Dharma Master Hsuan Tsang called him back,
saying something like, "Old Bodhisattva!" or "Dhy-
ana Companion!" or "Old Cultivator!" Those were
the standard forms of address at that time. He
said, "Don't go back into samadhi! It would be
better if you followed me to help propagate the
Buddhadharma. Although Shakyamuni Buddha, the Red
Yang Buddha, has already gone to Nirvana, his
Dharma is still in the world. Come along and help
me spread the teaching."

"How can I help propagate it?" asked the old
cultivator.

The Dharma Master said, "You go to Ch'ang An
and when you come to the house with the yellow-
tiled roof, get reborn there and you can eventually
help propagate the Dharma." That's because his present physical body was useless and he'd have to
trade it in on a new one. "You first go there and
get reborn and when I get back you can help me
propagate the Buddhadharma."

The old cultivator thought it over and agreed.
So the old cultivator went off to rebirth in Ch'ang
An and Dharma Master Hsuan Tsang went on his way
to India to bring back the Sutras. When he got
back, the first thing he did was congratulate the
Emperor on the birth of his son. "I sent you back
someone to be your son. That's been a happy event
indeed!"

But the Emperor said, "No. I didn't have a
son while you were away."

"No?" said the Dharma Master, and so he looked
into it and realized that the old cultivator had
gotten off the track and been reborn in the house
of the Defense Minister Yü Ch'ih Kung instead. Yü
Ch'ih Kung was tough and had a black face. He was
very talented and worked hard at his job, helping

the Emperor maintain the country and rule the empire. Probably the old cultivator was a bit sloppy when he did things, so although Dharma Master Hsuan Tsang had told him clearly to get born in the house with the yellow-tiled roof, the old fellow got it wrong, chose the one with the blue tiles, and ended up becoming the nephew of the flamboyant Defense Minister. Perhaps you can imagine what it was like being the nephew of Yü Ch'ih Kung. As soon as he was old enough, he took a tremendous fancy to eating meat, drinking wine, and entertaining women. Perhaps because he'd cultivated for kalpas, sitting in samadhi without ever coming out, he'd had a few false thoughts like, "Meat isn't bad as I recall. And I remember it was pleasant to drink wine. As for women, they weren't bad either." So when he took rebirth, he couldn't put down the contents of those three carts.

But as soon as Dharma Master Hsuan Tsang learned from the Emperor that there was no prince, he checked things out and knew that the old cultivator was in fact Yü Ch'ih Kung's nephew. So he approached the Defense Minister and said, "You know, there's someone in your family whom I sent here to help propagate the Buddhadharma."

The Defense Minister said shortly, "Well, you told him to come, so you tell him to go." So he was told, but he wouldn't go.

Finally Dharma Master Hsuan Tsang related the causes and conditions to Emperor T'ai Tsung who said immediately, "I'll issue an Imperial Command and order him to leave home."

"Fine," said Master Hsuan Tsang. "But it's likely he'll want to make it conditional. Whatever conditions he demands, just agree to them."

The Emperor affirmed and thereupon commanded the nephew of Yü Ch'ih Kung to appear in court for an audience. "You must leave home," was the Emperor's order.

"If I want to leave home I will, and if I don't want to leave home, I won't."

"This is a royal command and if you don't obey it, you will be beheaded."

That put a scare into the nephew and so he complied, but he still had the nerve to set up three conditions. "I want a cart of meat, a cart of wine, and a cart of women to follow me wherever I go."

"Agreed," said the Emperor. So it was decided and the nephew headed for Ta Hsing Shan--"Great Flourishing Goodness"--Monastery to leave the home-life. Since he was the son of an official, there was quite a fanfare and as the procession neared the temple gates, the big bell was rung and the gigantic drum was beaten to welcome him. As soon as he heard the bell and drum he opened enlightenment and said, "Oh, that's the way it is. To start with I was an old cultivator on that mountain." With a flick of his hand he waved away the carts, "Take them back. I don't want them anymore." But although he dismissed the carts upon leaving home, still people called him the "Three Cart Patriarch."

* * *

SHASTRA

Text:

As the World Honored One has said, "All dharmas have no self."

Commentary:

Now we begin the discussion of the Shastra proper. AS indicates that what is about to be said is a quote from the World Honored One himself. And who is THE WORLD HONORED ONE? "World Honored One" is one of the Ten Titles of a Buddha. It represents how the Buddha is "honored in the world and beyond the world." It is used here instead of the word "Buddha" to enhance the literary quality of the Chinese text, which in general uses four-character phrases.

The Buddha HAS SAID, "ALL DHARMAS HAVE NO SELF." All dharmas must be without "self".

"But why?" one wonders. "They obviously are in existence--real and actual. Why did the Buddha say that they are devoid of 'self'? The 'self' is truly and actually present, so why is it said there should be no 'self'?"

You say that the "self"--your "self"--is truly and actually present? Let us suppose that is so.

But then when you die, the corpse is still your
same old body. Where did the "self" of you go off
to? If when you die the "self" disappears, then
how can there actually be a "self" when you are
still alive? There's a problem inherent in your
supposition.
     The Buddha talked about all dharmas, but qual-
ified it by saying that all dharmas have to be
without a "self". There should not be a self.
You shouldn't be like people who do not understand
the Dharma and yet brag, "I lectured such-and-
such a Sutra," thrusting the "self" out in front.
Recently when we set thirty-six pigeons free, two
of them stayed. Why are they pigeons at all now?
It's just because of clinging to a "self". Before,
when they were people, they didn't listen to the
Dharma spoken by the Buddha and didn't understand.
Because they clung to "self" instead of being able
to be without a "self" they wound up being birds.
     The Shastra begins by quoting the Buddha, say-
ing, "All dharmas have no 'self'." The "self" he
refers to here means a view of self. It does not
refer to one's own body. There shouldn't be any
view of self. In the *Vajra Sutra* the Buddha spoke
about a view of self, a view of others, a view of
living beings and a view of a lifespan. One should
not have any of those views.
     Not only should one not have a "self," there
shouldn't even be any dharmas. All dharmas, as
well, do not exist. And if no dharmas exist, even
less does a "self" exist. Because of that, people
who cultivate the Way should get to the point of
having no self, and then each and every dharma is
perfected. If one can truly be without self, then
all dharmas interpenetrate without obstruction.
Whatever dharma one takes up does not fail to be
the Dharma Realm. Each has the nature of the
Dharma Realm, and all dharmas then appear before
one. Although all dharmas manifest, one should
be so there also are no dharmas. The Wonderful
is just at that point, and the difficulty is also
right at that point. For all dharmas whatsoever
to manifest before one and yet for one to have no
attachments to any dharmas means that one has
emptied dharmas of all marks. There aren't any
marks of dharmas at all. When one gets to that
point, then one really experiences true interpene-

tration without obstruction and one obtains incred-
ible freedom and ease. If one can be without
"self" then one will have freedom; but if one can't
manage to get rid of the self, one won't be able to
be free. It is that important.

Yet, how can one not have a self? It isn't
easy. One may think, "Here I am listening to the
Sutra being lectured, and how can you tell me that
I don't have a 'self'--that I'm not really here?"
I repeat, if you can be here listening to the Sutra and yet not know that you are here listening
to the Sutra--forgetting about people and having
no ego, emptying your "self" so there is no self
and there are no dharmas, so people and dharmas are
both empty--then you will be truly free and at ease.
But your attachments keep you from being devoid of
"self." What are you attached to? You are attached to the Five Skandhas--form, feeling, thinking, activity, and consciousness. You reckon the
form body which houses the Five Skandhas--this
false "self"--to be your "self." But actually, I
just refuted that by pointing out that when you
die it is still your body, but it doesn't have any
awareness, and so where did the "self" go? Your
"self" is huge--like Mount Sumeru. When you die,
where does it go? You don't know. Wouldn't you
say that's pitiful?

Those of externalist ways are attached to a
"great self," a "small self," and a"spiritual self"
in between. They've got a whole bunch of selves.
They say the "great self" is such that there's
nothing greater and the "small self" is such that
there's nothing smaller. This part of their theories has no use. The only part that makes any
sense is the "spiritual self" they speak of, for
there *is* a spiritual self. But those of externalist ways become attached to that spiritual self,
so it ends up being just another attachment.

Those of the Small Vehicle--the Two Vehicles
--also have their attachments. They have an attachment to a lopsided view of Nirvana, and call
that extreme view the "self." Bodhisattvas, too,
have attachments. What are their attachments?
They are attached to the existence of living beings
who can be crossed over, to a Buddha-Way which can
be sought, and to a True Suchness to which they
certify. Their certification has not reached the
point of being no knowing and no attaining. They

still have something to which they certify--some-
thing that they attain. They certify and attain
True Suchness. Since Bodhisattvas have these attachments, they also haven't forgotten the "self."
    As long as one has a "self," one still has
falseness. In the Buddhadharma, one wants to be
without a "self" in one's cultivation of all dharmas. Then one can obtain the state of the Great
Vehicle.
    The Shastra begins with this quotation of
what was spoken by the Buddha that "All dharmas
have no self." The subsequent text was written by
Heavenly Relative Bodhisattva.

Text:

What are all dharmas, and what is meant by
having no self? All dharmas may be generally
grouped into five categories:

Commentary:

    WHAT ARE ALL DHARMAS, AND WHAT IS MEANT BY HAVING NO
SELF? Now Heavenly Relative Bodhisattva will ana-
lyze the Buddha's words. ALL DHARMAS MAY BE GENERALLY
GROUPED INTO FIVE CATEGORIES. This is looking at them
from a broad and comprehensive viewpoint. What
are the Five Categories?

Text:

One, Mind Dharmas.

Commentary:

    The first ONE, MIND DHARMAS, means dharmas of
the Mind King. The mind is called the King because
each and every dharma is established based upon the
mind. If there were no mind dharmas, then no
dharmas would exist at all.
    It is said:

            The Buddha spoke all dharmas
                due to the minds of all living beings.

> If it weren't for all those minds,
> of what use would all dharmas be?

There are Eight Mind-King Dharmas, but we won't talk about them yet because they will be discussed later.

Text:

TWO, DHARMAS INTERACTIVE WITH THE MIND.

Commentary:

There are two ways to interpret number TWO, DHARMAS INTERACTIVE WITH THE MIND. On the one hand they are "dharmas belonging to the mind," and on the other, they are "servants of the mind." They work for the mind. The mind is the King and the Dharmas Interactive with the Mind are its servants. But they are also like great ministers. A king does not enact his own orders. He uses those who interact with him to implement his commands. That is how these dharmas function in relation to the mind --they carry out the commands of the Mind King. They are also known as "enumerations of the mind," because they have a fixed number--there are fifty-one of them. Since they arise from the mind, they are of the same family as the mind--they belong to the mind.

Text:

THREE, FORM DHARMAS.

Commentary:

THREE, FORM DHARMAS, is the third category. Anything that has form and shape, that has a substantial aspect to it, is known as a Form Dharma. This does not just refer to color but also to their tangible form--their solid aspect. There are eleven Form Dharmas. They, too, will be discussed later on.

Text:

FOUR, DHARMAS NOT INTERACTIVE WITH THE MIND.

Commentary:

Category FOUR, DHARMAS NOT INTERACTIVE WITH THE MIND, is those that do not interact, do not work together with the dharmas of any of the other categories. These kinds of dharmas are produced from the mind, and also have shape or some other representative aspect to them. There are twenty-four such dharmas.

Text:

FIVE, UNCONDITIONED DHARMAS.

Commentary:

The previous four categories were all conditioned dharmas. This final category, number FIVE, is that of UNCONDITIONED DHARMAS. These are used in cultivation of the world-transcending Great Vehicle. The states they represent can be certified to if one cultivates transcendental dharmas.

We haven't said anything in detail about the five categories of dharmas, because they'll all be discussed in detail later when we come to them in the text.

To review, the first four categories are conditioned dharmas and the fifth is unconditioned dharmas. If one only knows about the first four kinds, then one is an ordinary person or an externalist. If one knows the dharmas of the last category—the unconditioned dharmas—then one resides in the one-sided emptiness of the Small Vehicle, which has not reached the state of the Great Vehicle. What is the state of the Great Vehicle?

Right in the midst of the conditioned
is the unconditioned.

It's right within conditioned dharmas that one sees unconditioned dharmas. It isn't that one leaves conditioned dharmas behind and finds other dharmas that are unconditioned. Rather, whether it's the conditioned or the unconditioned turns on just a single thought. If one can understand the unconditioned while in the midst of the conditioned, that is what is meant by being in the world while transcending the world. When one is like this, then while in the world one does not fight, is not greedy, has no impeding obstructions, and is free and at ease. One exists in a state of interpenetration and it is extremely blissful. To be right in the world and yet transcend the world is the state of a Great Vehicle Bodhisattva. If at that point one can progress further and use the principle of no self to cultivate courageously and vigorously, then one can obtain the fruition of Wonderful Enlightenment. That is an overall view of the five categories of dharmas.

Text:

They are in this sequence because the first are supreme, the second interact with the first, the third are the shadows manifest by the previous two, the fourth are the positions in which the previous three are not found, and the last are revealed by the previous four.

Commentary:

THE FIRST refers to the mind dharmas. They ARE SUPREME over all else, because the mind is King and all dharmas arise from it. THE SECOND INTERACT WITH THE FIRST. The second category is dharmas interactive with the mind. They obey the orders of the Mind King. THE THIRD ARE THE SHADOWS MANIFEST BY THE PREVIOUS TWO. Form Dharmas are the third category. The way that form dharmas come into being is from the shadows cast by the mind dharmas and the dharmas interactive with the mind. Therefore, form dharmas belong to the Marks Division of the Eighth Consciousness.

Two Divisions of
The Eighth Consciousness

1. Seeing Division
2. Marks Division

The Marks Division basically has no nature of its
own. We see all sorts of things as having shape
or form, marks, characteristics, but basically they
don't exist at all. It's just that the Eighth
Consciousness makes these appear.
     THE FOURTH ARE THE POSITIONS IN WHICH THE PREVIOUS
THREE ARE NOT FOUND. The fourth category is Dharmas
Not Interactive with the Mind. They are separate
from Mind Dharmas, Dharmas Interactive with the
Mind, and Form Dharmas.
     THE LAST ARE REVEALED BY THE PREVIOUS FOUR. Those
in the fifth category--Unconditioned Dharmas--are
extremely profound. There's no way one could understand them. But in order to attempt to understand them, one must make use of the Conditioned
Dharmas. The Unconditioned Dharmas are revealed
by the Conditioned Dharmas.
     THEY ARE IN THIS SEQUENCE. They go from Mind Dhar-
mas to Dharmas Interactive with the Mind to Form
Dharmas to Dharmas Not Interactive with the Mind
to Unconditioned Dharmas. They appear in that order BECAUSE of the reasons just given.

Text:

The first, MIND DHARMAS, include in general
eight: I. THE EYE CONSCIOUSNESS, II. THE EAR
CONSCIOUSNESS, III. THE NOSE CONSCIOUSNESS, IV.
THE TONGUE CONSCIOUSNESS, V. THE BODY CONSCIOUS-
NESS, VI. THE MIND CONSCIOUSNESS, VII. THE MANAS
CONSCIOUSNESS, VIII. THE ALAYA CONSCIOUSNESS.

Commentary:

Now, at last, we are going to discuss some
dharmas. THE FIRST, MIND DHARMAS, INCLUDE IN GENERAL
EIGHT.

The Eight MIND DHARMAS

1. eye consciousness (眼識) *cakshur-vijnana*
2. ear consciousness (耳識) *shrotra-vijnana*
3. nose consciousness (鼻識) *ghrana-vijnana*
4. tongue consciousness (舌識) *jihva-vijnana*
5. body consciousness (身識) *kaya-vijnana*
6. mind consciousness (意識) *mano-vijnana*
7. manas consciousness (末那識) *manas-vijnana*
8. alaya consciousness (阿賴耶識) *alaya-vijnana*

I. THE EYE CONSCIOUSNESS. We say that eyes can see, but it's not actually the eyes themselves that see. It is the eye consciousness which sees. II. THE EAR CONSCIOUSNESS. We say the ears can hear, but if you sliced off your ears and laid them aside, would they be able to hear of themselves? If you gouged out your eyes and set them aside would they be able to see? Could you say, "I'm not going to the movies, but I'll send my eyes along and they can take in the show." Obviously not. The eyes cannot see by themselves. It is the eye consciousness which does the seeing. And from where does the eye consciousness come? From the mind--the Mind King. The same is true for all the other consciousnesses as well: III. THE NOSE CONSCIOUSNESS, IV, THE TONGUE CONSCIOUSNESS, V. THE BODY CONSCIOUSNESS, and VI. THE MIND CONSCIOUSNESS. The way it works is that the six sense faculties of eyes, ears, nose, tongue, body, and mind combine with the six defiling sense objects of sights, sounds, smells, tastes, objects of touch and dharmas. When this occurs, between each pair a consciousness arises. On the inside there are six faculties, on the outside there are six sense objects, and in the middle, in between the faculties and their objects, the six consciousnesses arise. Taken together, these three sets of six make up the Eighteen Realms. I discussed these in detail when I lectured the *Heart Sutra,* so if you want to explore them more, you can look into that text.

The mind consciousness, the sixth or "intellectual" consciousness, is not really the mind, properly speaking. The Sixth consciousness is the function of the mind whose substance is the seventh consciousness, the MANAS CONSCIOUSNESS, also called the "transmitting" consciousness or the "defil-

ing" consciousness.   It is the substance of the
mind.   It continually takes the functions of the
sixth consciousness and transmits them to the eighth
consciousness,   THE ALAYA CONSCIOUSNESS. The eighth
consciousness is called the alaya, which means
"store," because it stores all information trans-
mitted to it by the seventh.   If it is turned
around, it becomes the nature of the Treasury of
the Thus Come One.
   When the Eight Consciousnesses are turned
around, they become the Four Wisdoms.

The Four Wisdoms

1. The Great Perfect Mirror Wisdom.
2. The Wisdom of Equality.
3. The Wisdom of Wonderful Contemplation.
4. The Wisdom that Accomplishes What is
   Done.

How does one turn them around? One must work hard
at cultivation and then one will know how to do it.
I can't tell you now because even if I were to tell
you, in the future you still wouldn't know.

   Upon awakening, one obtains them oneself.

If you yourself cultivate, then you yourself will
know.   Before you know, it doesn't do any good to
be told.   But after you know, you very naturally
will have the use of them.
   The alaya is the store consciousness because
it is like the ground in   which we plant seeds,
storing them away until they sprout.   That is why
there are often analogies made likening the mind
to the ground.   For instance it is said,

   Plant the mind-ground and
   Nourish the divine nature.

All the different external and internal states we
experience, whether good or bad, defiled or pure,
are planted in the eighth consciousness.   The seeds
of every event, circumstance, and experience are
stored away in that consciousness.   If you cultivate and turn that store consciousness around, then
it becomes the nature of the Treasury of the Thus
Come One.   It's just a matter of being able to use

it. If you can use it, then the Great Perfect Mirror Wisdom will appear. If you can't use it, then
you just keep on having false thinking. And all
the false thoughts you have, whether you act upon
them or not, still get stored in the eighth consciousness. Even the most subtle kinds of mental
activities--thoughts which you are completely un-
aware of--get stored there. Despite your lack of
awareness of them, the seeds are planted there just
the same.

  In a single unenlightened thought, the
   Three Subtle Marks appear.

The Three Subtle Marks are the Mark of Karma, the
Mark of Turning, and the Mark of Manifesting. When
they appear, the Thus Come One's Treasury turns
into the eighth consciousness. However, if you
are able to turn that eighth consciousness around
to become the nature of the Treasury of the Thus
Come One, then you are one who has returned to the
origin and gone back to the source.

  Very generally speaking, that's what the Eight
Mind Dharmas are like. If discussed in detail it
gets incredibly complex.

  We have just introduced the Eight Mind Dharmas.
But why is it that the sixth is called the manas--
"mind," or "intellectual" consciousness and so is
the seventh? It is because the sixth relies on
the seventh, for the seventh is the root or basis
of the mind consciousness. It is the substance of
the mind and the sixth is the function of the mind,
as was already mentioned. The seventh consciousness is called the "defiled consciousness." It's
also known as "that upon which the defiled and the
pure rely." The sixth consciousness is also defiled and the eighth consciousness is fundamentally
pure. Both the sixth and the eighth rely on the
seventh consciousness. That explains this name
for it.

  The eighth consciousness is the alaya, which
means "non-vanishing". It also translates as
"store". "Non-vanishing" means that True Suchness
accords with birth and death and yet remains without vanishing. This consciousness is never lost.
It doesn't disappear. "Store" consciousness has
three meanings.

*The Three Meanings of
Store Consciousness*

1. That which stores.
2. That which is stored.
3. Attaching and storing.

It is "that which stores," because it stores all good and evil seeds within it. It is "that which is stored" because it is comprised of those seeds stored in it. All good and evil karma is stored here. It also means "attaching and storing," for attachment and storing take place within the eighth consciousness, because absolutely every thought we have, be it a good one or a bad one, is stored in the eighth consciousness. All dharmas are manifestations of the eighth consciousness. The things that we see comprise the Marks Division of the Eighth Consciousness. Our ability to see them makes up the Seeing Division of the Eighth Consciousness. That's why it is said that the myriad dharmas are consciousness only. That is, they arise only from the mind. Consciousness is just True Suchness when it is bound. Therefore, this consciousness is what we refer to as the Buddha Nature. It is the source of all good and evil. It is the original home of all sages and ordinary people.

Text:

The second, DHARMAS INTERACTIVE WITH THE MIND, include, in general, fifty-one. They are divided into six categories: I. THE FIVE UNIVERSALLY INTERACTIVE, II. THE FIVE PARTICULAR STATES, III. THE ELEVEN WHOLESOME, IV. THE SIX FUNDAMENTAL AFFLICTIONS, V. THE TWENTY DERIVATIVE AFFLICTIONS, AND VI. THE FOUR UNFIXED.

I. THE FIVE UNIVERSALLY INTERACTIVE are: 1. ATTENTION, 2. CONTACT, 3. FEELING, 4. CONCEPTUALIZATION, AND 5. DELIBERATION.

Commentary:

Now we will discuss THE SECOND, DHARMAS INTERAC-
TIVE WITH THE MIND. These are also mind dharmas, but
they are those which belong to the mind, not the
Mind King. The Mind King is the eighth consciousness. At any given moment the eighth consciousness
pervades the entire Dharma Realm. Fundamentally,
it doesn't have any wearisome defilements. It can
stop all karmic retribution. But those dharmas
which belong to the mind help the mind enact deeds
of good and evil, creating good or evil karma. The
Mind King is like an emperor. Just as the emperor
orders his ministers to carry out his commands, so,
too, the Mind King relies on the Dharmas Interactive with the Mind in order to get things done.
In this case, there are IN GENERAL, FIFTY-ONE. They
are also known as "servants of the mind." They
are also called "enumerations of the mind," because
the mind has so many of these kinds of delibera-
tions that they could never be counted. But there
are fifty-one enumerations of the mind which are
most important. These Fifty-One Dharmas Interactive with the Mind are further grouped into Six
Divisions.

Fifty-One DHARMAS
INTERACTIVE WITH THE MIND

(心所有法) *caitasika dharmah*

The SIX DIVISIONS

   I. Five Universally Interactive
      (遍行) *sarvatraga*
  II. Five Particular States (別境) *viniyata*
 III. Eleven Wholesome (善) *kushala*
  IV. Six Fundamental Afflictions
      (根本煩惱) *klesha*
   V. Twenty Derivative (Subsidiary)
      Afflictions (隨煩惱) *upaklesha*
  VI. Four Unfixed (不定) *aniyata*

These Six Divisions are like departments. The
Universally Interactive Dharmas are called that because they pervade all places. They operate universally, and there are five specific dharmas
listed in this division. Particular States Dharmas
are individualized. Whereas the Universally Interactive Dharmas pervaded all places, these Particular States don't pervade at all. They are
isolated. They are very special, solitary, and
individual states. There are also five of these
listed. Of the Wholesome Dharmas, eleven specific
ones are listed.

Afflictions are the next division. We talk
about having afflictions, but now we will learn
more specifically just what afflictions are, along
with Derivative Afflictions as well. There are
Six Fundamental, or major, Afflictions and Twenty
Derivative Afflictions which will each be introduced. The Derivative Afflictions are subdivided
into small, medium, and large afflictions. Last,
there are Four Unfixed Universally Interactive
Dharmas.

I. FIVE UNIVERSALLY INTERACTIVE DHARMAS

1. Attention (作意) *manaskara*
2. Contact (觸) *sparsha*
3. Feeling (受) *vedana*
4. Conceptualization (想) *samjna*
5. Deliberation (思) *cetana*

1. ATTENTION is as when paying attention, putting one's mind's attention on something, or literally "making a mind." Attention is an attempt
to grasp onto a state. Basically, the Mind King
does not enter into this act of attention by itself. But because of good and evil karma planted
as seeds in the eighth consciousness from long-
distant kalpas to the present, the eighth consciousness becomes permeated by these habitual tendencies,
just as smoke permeates food being cured or incense

permeates the atmosphere of the Buddhahall. When
the permeation reaches a saturation point, movement
arises within the eighth consciousness. That movement takes the form of attention. Therefore, attention marks the beginning of the mind giving
rise to states.

The state of a Bodhisattva is such that he
does not have to perform the act of attention in
order to know something. He can know good and
evil causes and effects without making an effort
to do so. Arhats, however, do have to perform the
act of attention. They must pay attention to see
what's going on. Once they have gone through the
process of attention, then they can know what something is all about. They can know the causes and
results of any given situation that occurs.

For example, why did the thirty-four pigeons
fly away? Basically, it is because when they were
people they created certain kinds of karma. They
didn't work hard at their cultivation. They thought
they would leave home, but they never did. They
thought they would get around to cultivating, but
they never did. They thought they would become
vegetarians, but they never did. They thought they
would recite the Buddha's name, but they never did.
They never got around to doing what they were supposed to be doing.

This does not apply just to pigeons. Some
people who come to the Buddhist Lecture Hall never
leave. Others come but don't stay. Still others
intend to come but never make it in the door. You
shouldn't look upon these conditions as ordinary--
nothing special--and take them for granted. They
are, in fact, quite extraordinary. People without
good roots simply cannot get themselves inside the
door of the Buddhist Lecture Hall. If the people
here didn't have good roots, they wouldn't be able
to listen to the Sutras. All those who are able
to listen to Sutras have good roots. However, even
then, there are great good roots and small good
roots; there are those with many good roots and
those with few good roots. If you want to bring
forth the resolve for Bodhi, you must listen to
more and more Dharma. When you come to understand
a lot of Buddhadharma, then very naturally, you
will resolve your mind on Bodhi. The first Universally Interactive Dharma is attention.

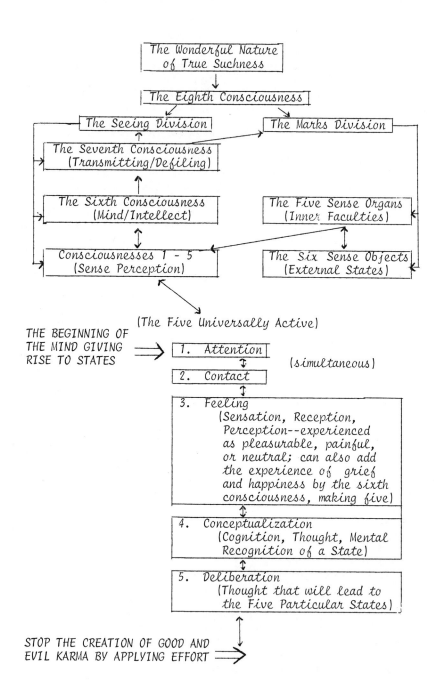

The Wonderful Nature
of True Suchness

↓

The Eighth Consciousness

The Seeing Division

The Marks Division

The Seventh Consciousness
(Transmitting/Defiling)

The Sixth Consciousness
(Mind/Intellect)

The Five Sense Organs
(Inner Faculties)

Consciousnesses 1 - 5
(Sense Perception)

The Six Sense Objects
(External States)

(The Five Universally Active)

THE BEGINNING OF
THE MIND GIVING
RISE TO STATES
→

1. Attention

(simultaneous)

2. Contact

3. Feeling
    (Sensation, Reception,
    Perception--experienced
    as pleasurable, painful,
    or neutral; can also add
    the experience of grief
    and happiness by the sixth
    consciousness, making five)

4. Conceptualization
    (Cognition, Thought, Mental
    Recognition of a State)

5. Deliberation
    (Thought that will lead to
    the Five Particular States)

STOP THE CREATION OF GOOD AND
EVIL KARMA BY APPLYING EFFORT →

CONTACT is the second one, but it is also what the remaining three Universally Interactive Dharmas rely upon. Once contact is established, FEELING arises. Once feeling arises, CONCEPTUALIZATION occurs. Once there is conceptualization, then DELIBERATION sets in. Contact provides the place for feeling, conceptualization, and deliberation to arise. Deliberation is the process of reckoning, or judging. Thoughts like, "How can I get that state? What about this?" fall into this category.

Universally Interactive Dharmas pervade the Three Natures and extend throughout the Three Periods of Time.

The Three Natures

1. The Good Nature
2. The Evil Nature
3. The Indeterminate Nature

"Indeterminate" means it's not known whether it is good or evil.

The Three Periods of Time

1. Past
2. Present
3. Future

What is meant by "past"? What is meant by "present"? What is meant by "future"? I will tell you. Today is the present, yesterday was the past, and tomorrow is the future. The future, which hasn't come yet, doesn't exist because it hasn't come. The present keeps changing and does not stop, so it doesn't exist either. The past is already gone, so it doesn't exist. Therefore, ultimately, the Three Periods of time cannot be got at.

If one could put a stop to the Five Kinds of Universally Interactive Dharmas--which one *can* do whenever one wants--then one wouldn't create evil karma. But if you don't stop them, they continue to exist. Actually, with the coming into being of the Five Universally Interactive Dharmas, one still hasn't created any good or evil karma. It is when the Five Particular States arise that there is no stopping the creation of good and evil karma. So, stopping the process at the level of the Universally Interactive Dharmas prevents the creation of good and evil karma.

Text:

The FIVE PARTICULAR STATES are: 1. Desire, 2. RESOLUTION, 3. RECOLLECTION, 4. Concentration, and 5. JUDGMENT.

Commentary:

"Particular" can have several meanings, such as "special," "discriminated," and "individual." The word "particular" is used to describe these dharmas in order to indicate their difference from the Five Universally Interactive. The Five Universally Interactive Dharmas are such that each one of them includes the other four. But the FIVE PARTICULAR STATES dharmas are not the same as each other and are, in fact, quite distinct and individual, making them just the opposite of the previous group of five. Each of these Five Particular States dharmas acts upon the conditions that occur when a certain state arises. The mind that "climbs on conditions" involves itself with the conditions of a state that arises.[1] It is that function of

---

[1] "Climbing on conditions" (攀緣) is alambana in Sanskrit and means "support," in this case for a thought or mental process. The Chinese use of the word "conditions" (緣) to describe the action of the mind on a dharma comes from this meaning. But in English we cannot say the mind "conditions" a dharma, for in fact it is dharmas which "condition mind." The mind "thinks" dharmas in the same way that other senses respond to their corresponding sense objects. "Climbing on conditions" means "taking advantage of," referring to the various ways in which the mind sets up factors that make states arise or act as a support for those states.

"climbing on conditions that causes these Five
Particular States to arise. As has already been
mentioned, at the level of the Five Universally
Interactive Dharmas, thoughts of good and evil have
not yet formed. At that point, one could stop the
mind processes and thereby keep such thoughts from
being produced. If one works hard at cultivating
these dharmas, one can keep from producing thoughts
of good and evil. If one can manage not to produce
thoughts of good and evil, then there will not be
any creation of good or evil karma. However, if
one gives rise to these Five Particular States
dharmas which are also among the Dharmas Interactive with the Mind, then one can no longer stop
thoughts of good and evil from arising. Therefore,
the actual "doing" of good and evil begins with
these Five Particular States.

THE FIVE PARTICULAR STATES

1. Desire (欲) *chanda*
2. Resolution (勝解) *adhimoksha*
3. Recollection (念) *smriti*
4. Concentration (三麼地) *samadhi*
5. Judgment (慧) *prajna*

What is meant by DESIRE? It is a want for
something. Once one wants something, the next
thing that happens is that one tries to get it--
to grasp at it. That is the result of desire.
Wha, does one want to get most? Pleasurable states.
One wants to have pleasurable experiences.

RESOLUTION is rendered in Chinese by the
two characters that mean literally "supreme understanding." This mental dharma functions when a
state arises that one wants to investigate, to
figure out. One becomes involved in a state and
becomes determined to figure it out, to understand
what it is all about. One becomes quite intent
upon this, thinking things like, "What shall I do
about it? I've got to come to terms with this and
figure it out." One feels one *must* make up one's
mind about it and know exactly what's going on with
it. When one is intent upon this process of resolution, if other causes and conditions arise during
that time, they won't be able to shake one's mind
or prevent it from making this resolution. That's
why the Chinese   uses "supreme understanding," to
try and indicate the intensity behind this dharma
of resolution.

RECOLLECTION means "remembering clearly." What
does one remember clearly? One remembers the
states one has already experienced. For example,
an adult may be able to recollect what he studied
in grammar school. That's an example of this
dharma--clearly remembering and not forgetting--
which is the third Particular State.

Although the Sanskrit for the next dharma is
samadhi, what is being described is not the samadhi
as defined in the list of Precepts, Samadhi, and
Wisdom--the Three Non-Outflow Studies. Here we
will render the word in English as CONCENTRATION,
because it means to exclusively pay attention to
something. It means to be without distractions in
one's mind. It means to continually think about
something or to focus one's attention on something.
When this dharma is functioning, your mind will be
concentrated on one particular experience to the
exclusion of all others. However, this kind of
concentration is that which an ordinary person is
capable of. One uses it when performing some activity which one wants to bring to successful ac-
complishment. Sometimes, with that much concentration an accuracy of judgment will arise, which
is the fifth Particular State.

Although the Sanskrit renders the fifth dharma
Prajna, it is not referring to real wisdom, but to
an ability which the average person possesses. It
is not the Prajna wisdom which people who cultivate the Way are working to bring forth. Here,
we will term it JUDGMENT, for it refers to being
worldly wise which involves the ability to make
judgments and decisions--to have a "sense of judgment." It functions when one tries to figure out if
something one did was correct or incorrect. Or
when one wishes to do something one may use this
dharma to determine if what one wishes to do is
possible or impossible. Having done something,
one may then think, "Did I do that right? Was
that good or not? Should I have done that or not?"
Therefore, judgment is a worldly dharma.

When discussing world-transcending dharmas,
we can refer to samadhi and Prajna, and they are
dharmas which help each other out. Samadhi gives
rise to Prajna wisdom and Prajna wisdom enhances
samadhi. That's how samadhi and wisdom work on
the world-transcending level. But when we speak
of concentration and judgment, we are talking about
worldly dharmas, worldly wisdom, and these remain
isolated from each other. They do not function
simultaneously. It's not the case that if one has
concentration then one will have judgment or if
one has judgment one will have concentration. These
worldly dharmas of concentration and judgment cannot happen at the same time. When one is in the
midst of concentration, one will not be using the
dharma of judgment and when one is in the process
of using judgment, one will not be simultaneously
using concentration. At the worldly level these
two dharmas are separate--isolated from each other.

All of these Five Particular States are the
same way--isolated from each other. Each one
deals with its own particular state. It's not that
each one pervades the other four as with the previous Universally Interactive Dharmas. The Five
Particular States are different states altogether.
Since they aren't the same, let us look at how
each arises. "Desire" arises for pleasurable
states. In states requiring decisiveness, "resolution" is used. Towards states one has already
experienced one uses "recollection." "Concentra-

tion" is produced towards states which one wishes
to contemplate. "Judgment" is used to make deter-
minations about states which arise. These, then,
are the Five Particular States.

Text:

III. THE ELEVEN WHOLESOME DHARMAS are:
1. FAITH, 2. VIGOR, 3. SHAME, 4. REMORSE, 5. AB-
SENCE OF GREED, 6. ABSENCE OF ANGER, 7. ABSENCE OF
STUPIDITY, 8. LIGHT EASE, 9. NON-LAXNESS, 10. RE-
NUNCIATION, 11. NON-HARMING.

Commentary:

This is the third of the Six Divisions of
Dharmas Interactive with the Mind. These WHOLESOME
DHARMAS are good. They can help you cultivate and
accomplish your work.

The ELEVEN WHOLESOME DHARMAS

1. Faith (信) *shraddha*
2. Vigor (精進) *virya*
3. Shame (慚) *hri*
4. Remorse (愧) *apatrapya*
5. Absence of Greed (無貪) *alobha*
6. Absence of Anger (無瞋) *advesha*
7. Absence of Stupidity (無癡) *amoha*
8. Light Ease (輕安) *prashrabdhi*
9. Non-laxness (不放逸) *apramada*
10. Renunciation (行捨) *upeksha*
11. Non-Harming (不害) *ahimsa*

1. FAITH is necessary in whatever it is one
does. One needs to have a sense of belief, an
attitude of faith. First one needs to have faith
in oneself. What kind of faith? One needs to
have faith that one certainly can become a Buddha.
One has to believe that there's no difference between the Buddha and oneself. But that lack of
difference is in the Buddha nature. Cultivation
is still required in order to actually become a
Buddha. If one cultivates, one will become a

Buddha. In order to do so, one must have an initial belief in that principle.

Second, not only does one want to believe that one can become a Buddha oneself, but to also believe that all people can become Buddhas. However, not only can all people become Buddhas, one should believe that all living beings have the Buddha nature and are capable of becoming Buddhas. If one has that kind of faith, then one should begin by following the rules oneself. To follow the rules means to hold the precepts. First one holds the precepts and then one can become a Buddha. So one does that oneself and also encourages others to do so as well.

Faith must be solid, like a rock, firm and sturdy. Faith shouldn't be like a pile of ashes which seems to have some substance to it, but which crumbles at the slightest disturbance. Don't be too soft. One's faith must be strong and solid.

Once one has faith, then one should put it into action with VIGOR. What should one be vigorous doing? One should be vigorous in cultivating. Be mindful of the Buddha, mindful of the Dharma, and mindful of the Sangha. Use vigor in doing that. Don't always be retreating. One should always keep advancing, being more and more vigorous.

The third Wholesome Dharma is SHAME, which also carries the meaning of "repentance." This dharma is enacted with regard to one's self. One brings forth an attitude of shame and repentance, thinking, "The things I have done are really not right. I ought to change and become a new person."

Number four is REMORSE. This dharma is enacted with regard to others. One should harbor a sense of remorse akin to embarrassment, thinking, "I'm not up to that person. I shouldn't feel that I am better than other people. That person is actually much better than I am. See how that person is always in such good spirits and free from worry? Why is it that I have so many worries?" That is the kind of attitude involved in remorse.

Dharmas five, six, and seven of the Eleven Wholesome Dharmas are called the Three Kinds of Good Roots, and are the opposite of the Three poisons.

The Three Poisons

1. Greed
2. Anger
3. Stupidity

The Three Kinds of Good Roots

1. Absence of Greed
2. Absence of Anger
3. Absence of Stupidity

1. ABSENCE OF GREED means it is wholesome not to be greedy. The way greed works is that if there's something one hasn't gotten, then one wants to get it. But after getting it, one fears losing it. Both the desire to obtain and the fear of losing are aspects of greed. Therefore, don't be greedy for wealth, don't be greedy for beautiful forms, don't be greedy for fame, and don't be greedy for profit.

I teach you not to be greedy, but I, myself, must be greedy. However, I'm being greedy on your behalf. I'm greedy for everyone else's sake, not for my own sake. The greed that I have exists on behalf of all cultivators in America. What is it I'm greedy for? I'm greedy for a Way-place--a pure place you in America can cultivate in. If you don't even have a Way-place, how can you cultivate the Way? To have the Way, you must have a place. So, I've become greedy for a Way-place and now it is about to appear as a response to my greed. To begin with, I wasn't going to get greedy, but I see that if I'm not, your opportunities for becoming Buddhas will evolve a lot more slowly. So that's the motivation behind my greed--that all of you can become Buddhas a little sooner. All of you should help me out with this greed of mine. I just told you not to be greedy and now I'm telling you to be greedy! But this greed is for the sake of others, so don't hesitate to have more of this kind of greed.

If one is greedy for oneself, one is indeed greedy, but if one is greedy for the sake of living beings, one is not greedy. However, a certain fault can develop out of this. It's very easy for people to become hypocritical, rationalizing that what they want is for the sake of all beings when

in fact what they want is for their own sakes.
People who have this fault can be very clever in
instigating it, so that others fail to recognize
the real motives behind one's greed. As long as
it's for the sake of oneself, it's still greed.
What exactly is meant by having it be not for oneself? If one does not seek fame for oneself, if
one does not seek profit for oneself, if one does
not seek any kind of self-benefit, then what one
is doing is not for oneself.

Why is greed considered unwholesome? It is
a defiled kind of dharma. It is unclean. Anyone
who is greedy, therefore, is also unclean. One
has defilement and filth and one has attachments.
That is why greed isn't good. Retributions involv-
ing suffering come as a result of having been
greedy in the past.

The sixth Wholesome Dharma is ABSENCE OF ANGER.
Anger   is harbored within. It is a kind of hos-
tility. An absence of anger, then, is when one
does not get angry even when someone else gets
angry at one or opposes one.

An ABSENCE OF STUPIDITY is the seventh. Stupidity is submerged darkness. It is a lack of bright-
ness--ignorance. Absence of greed, anger, and
stupidity are the Three Kinds of Good Roots.

LIGHT EASE is an initial expedient in the cultivation of Ch'an Samadhi. Before Samadhi is actually achieved, one experiences this kind of light
ease in the process of cultivation. Where does
this state come from? It comes from being vigorous
in cultivating wholesome dharmas and in stopping
evil dharmas. In addition to being vigorous in
wholesome dharmas, one must add the Three Kinds of
Good Roots just discussed. Then the merit and
virtue one receives will take the form of light
ease, which is an incredibly comfortable feeling
experienced by both body and mind. Whenever one
sits in meditation investigating Ch'an, one has an
unsurpassed happiness; an extremely blissful state
arises.

The ninth Wholesome Dharma is NON-LAXNESS. Not
being lax means following the rules. If one is
not lax, one is following the rules and relying on
the Dharma to cultivate. To never be casual or
nonchalant at any time is what it means to not be
lax. What is an example of being lax? Remember
how at the start of the first summer session one

of my disciples used to take his legs out of full
lotus, stretch them out full length and prop them
on a cushion while the Sutra lecture was in progress? That's an example of being lax. Now, however, he doesn't do that, which is an example of
non-laxness.

RENUNCIATION, the tenth Wholesome Dharma, specifically refers to renouncing everything within the
activity skandha which is not in accord with the
rules. The kind of renunciation one does with regard to the activity skandha is different from the
renunciation that takes place with regard to the
feeling skandha. Renunciations within the feeling
skandha are made as soon as one becomes enlightened. But renunciation within the activity skandha is not so obvious. We know that the activity
skandha involves a non-stop flow of thoughts.
Within this, one must renounce everything that
arises which is not in accord with the rules. For
every little bit which is renounced, one comes
that much closer to a response with the Way. If
in every thought one is capable of this kind of
renunciation, then in every thought one enters
the Way.

The last of the Wholesome Dharmas is NON-HARMING.
This means not harming any living being. "Absence
of Anger" is different from "Non-Harming." Absence of Anger involves not reciprocating when
someone else directs anger at one, or shows hostil-
ity towards one, or doesn't do what one wants him
to do. It is a passive stance. But Non-Harming
is a restraint on one's own aggressive tendencies.
It refers to how one treats others, specifically
by not harming them.

Text:

IV. THE SIX FUNDAMENTAL AFFLICTIONS are:
1. GREED, 2. ANGER, 3. STUPIDITY, 4. ARROGANCE,
5. DOUBT, and 6. IMPROPER VIEWS.

Commentary:

These are THE SIX FUNDAMENTAL AFFLICTIONS. They
can also be grouped as Ten Afflictions, because

they include the Five Dull Servants and the Five
Sharp Servants.

The Five Dull Servants

1. Greed
2. Anger
3. Stupidity
4. Arrogance
5. Doubt

The Five Sharp Servants

1. View of a Body
2. Extreme Views
3. View of Grasping at Precepts
   and Prohibitions
4. View of Grasping at Views
5. Deviant Views

The first five of the Six Fundamental Afflictions correspond to the Five Dull Servants. The
sixth of the Six Fundamental Afflictions corres-
ponds to the Five Sharp Servants. In other words,
there are five kinds of improper views.

"Dull" describes how these "servants," or
"causes" are slow to come on. They incapacitate
one so that one becomes slow and sluggish, unable
to understand what's going on, and inept at making
decisions. "Sharp" describes how these five views
cause one to act very fast and jump to conclusions.

THE SIX FUNDAMENTAL AFFLICTIONS

1. Greed (貪) *raga*
2. Anger (瞋) *pratigha*
3. Stupidity (癡) *moha*
4. Arrogance (慢) *mana*
5. Doubt (疑) *vicikitsa*
6. Improper Views (不正見) *drishti*

The first of the Six Fundamental Afflictions
is GREED. Greed is insatiable. There is greed for
wealth, sex, fame, food, and sleep and there is
greed for forms, sounds, smells, tastes, and objects of touch.

The second of the Fundamental Afflictions is ANGER.
Being greedy and then not obtaining the object of

one's greed leads one to give rise to anger. When
things don't go the way one wants them to, one gets
angry. Once anger arises, STUPIDITY results. That
is the third Fundamental Affliction. It is a lack
of clarity, a confusion which causes one to do improper things. There's no telling what someone who
is stupid might do--just about *anything*.

The fourth Fundamental Affliction is ARROGANCE.
That is pride and conceit which causes one to look
down on others. It is a supercilious attitude.

The fifth is DOUBT. When something comes up,
one cannot make up one's mind about it. One is
never quite sure about it. One never knows quite
what to think.

The sixth is IMPROPER VIEWS. As mentioned, this
one Fundamental Affliction divides into five parts.

(1) The View of a Body. One is attached to
one's own body as being "me" or "mine." One attaches to the body as belonging to oneself and
further attaches to possessions.

(2) Extreme Views. This is being prejudiced
to one extreme or another. If one doesn't lean
too far to the left, then one leans too far to the
right. If one doesn't go too far, one doesn't come
far enough. One is not in accord with the Middle
Way.

(3) The View of Grasping at Views. This is
the deviant view of mistaking what is not a result
to be a result. For example, people with this kind
of view may claim to have attained some kind of
fruit of cultivation when in fact they have not.

(4) View of Grasping at Precepts and Prohibitions. This is the observance of precepts that
one shouldn't observe. For instance, in India
there are those who observe the precepts--the be-
havior--of cows and dogs. In doing this, one mistakes what is not a cause for a cause. Basically,
something was not a proper cause, but with this
kind of view a person will mistake it for a cause.

(5) Deviant Views. People with deviant knowledge and deviant views will not speak proper
Dharma, even if they are capable of it and others
want them to. But if asked to talk about defiled
dharmas, they will always do so, particularly discussing the affairs between men and women. They
will talk about what men are like and what women
are like, and say things like "You don't need to
hold the precepts; only stupid people hold precepts.

People with wisdom don't need to hold them." They
keep talking until eventually their listeners who
originally did not harbor thoughts of desire or
have defiled thinking, will be caused to give rise
to them. Someone may have been just on the verge
of obtaining the states of the Dhyanas, having gotten rid of the "guest-dust"; but, encountering someone who discusses defiled things, that person lets
the "guest-dust" back in again and starts having
thoughts of desire.

So, when you lecture on the Sutras, whether
you are a left-home person or a layperson, a man
or woman, you should not discuss defiled dharmas.
You should speak about pure Dharmas. The six sense
faculties should be pure and you shouldn't cause
people to have desire. If in the course of lecturing on the Sutras you speak of defiled dharmas
and provoke desire in people, in the future you
will have a terrible retribution.

These Six Fundamental Afflictions are also
part of the Fifty-One Dharmas Interactive with the
Mind, as are the Twenty Derivative Afflictions
which come next. The twenty derive from the six.

TEXT:

V. THE TWENTY DERIVATIVE AFFLICTIONS are:
1. WRATH, 2. HATRED, 3. RAGE, 4. COVERING, 5. DE-
CEIT, 6. FLATTERY, 7. CONCEIT, 8. HARMING, 9.
JEALOUSY, 10. STINGINESS, 11. LACK OF SHAME,
12. LACK OF REMORSE, 13. LACK OF FAITH. 14. LAZI-
NESS, 15. LAXNESS, 16. TORPOR, 17. RESTLESSNESS,
18. DISTRACTION, 19. IMPROPER KNOWLEDGE, AND
20. SCATTEREDNESS.

Commentary:

These Twenty Afflictions are called "derivative," because they derive from the Six Fundamental
Afflictions. They divide into Three Grades.

The Three Grades of Derivative Afflictions

1. Major-Grade Derivative Afflictions
2. Intermediate-Grade Derivative Afflictions
3. Minor-Grade Derivative Afflictions

In addition, there are Three Factors which pertain to Derivative Afflictions.

The Three Factors Pertaining to Derivative Afflictions

1. Reinforcement by Types. Afflictions tend to arise together; therefore, they are grouped by type.

A. The Three Types of Derivative Afflictions

(1) Typical Major-Grade Afflictions
(2) Typical Intermediate-Grade Afflictions
(3) Typical Minor-Grade Afflictions

Reinforcement by types works for afflictions much the same as it does for people and creatures. It is said:

> People of the same type gather together.
> Creatures divide into their various
>   species and classes.

For instance, people who study the Buddhadharma gather together in one place. People who study demonic dharmas go to places where demonic dharmas are taught. People who want to learn worldly dharmas find a place where worldly dharmas can be studied. Creatures, too, band together in groups according to their species, and so forth. Their varieties and distinctions are inexpressibly many. The same principle holds true for the way in which Derivative Afflictions become grouped. For instance, Major-Grade type Afflictions tend to arise based on one another, and therefore simultaneously. The same is true for Intermediate and Minor-Grade type Afflictions.

2. *Pervasive Infection by the Unwholesome Nature.*
"Pervasive infection" means that the afflictions
penetratingly influence one another. For instance,
"lack of shame" also brings about "lack of remorse," because if one is not repentant, one will
also not feel remorseful. Another example is "lack
of faith," which gives rise in turn to "indolence,"
"laxness," and other derivative afflictions.
3. *Permeation by Two Defilements of the Mind.*

A. *The Two Defilements of the Mind*

(1) Covering Defilement
(2) Indeterminate Defilement.

"Covering" means keeping things hidden and not allowing anyone to know. "Indeterminate" means the
defilement cannot be categorized as to its relative goodness or evil.
    If all Three Factors are present, the afflic-
tion is a major-grade one. If two factors are
present, the affliction is an intermediate-grade
one. If none of the Three Factors is present, then
the affliction which has arisen is an isolated one
and is thus classed as a minor-grade affliction.

THE TWENTY DERIVATIVE AFFLICTIONS

A. *Ten Minor-Grade Afflictions*

1. Wrath (忿) *krodha*
2. Hatred (恨) *upanaha*
3. Rage (惱) *pradasa*
4. Covering (覆) *mraksha*
5. Deceit (誑) *maya*
6. Flattery (諂) *shathya*
7. Conceit (憍) *mada*
8. Harming (害) *vihimsa*
9. Jealousy (嫉) *irshya*
10. Stinginess (慳) *matsarya*

B. *The Two Intermediate-Grade Afflictions*

11. Lack of Shame (無慚) *ahrikya*
12. Lack of Remorse (無愧) *anapatrapya*

C. *The Eight Major-Grade Afflictions*

13. Lack of Faith (不信) *ashraddhya*
14. Indolence (懈怠) *kausidya*

15. Laxness (放逸) *pramada*
16. Torpor (昏沉) *styana*
17. Restlessness (掉舉) *auddhatya*
18. Distraction (失念) *mushitasmriti*
19. Improper Knowledge (不正知) *asamprajanya*
20. Scatteredness (散亂) *vikshepa*

First, we will discuss the Ten Minor Afflictions. 1. WRATH. Wrath occurs when a state arises which is in opposition to one's wishes. When something isn't going one's way, when something is really bothering one, when one becomes very emotional about something, then wrath can arise. It comes on suddenly and is a combination of anger and hatred--an unexpected and intense emotional reaction.

2. HATRED. This affliction occurs when one is faced with situations similar to the ones described above, but one does not resort to wrath. Instead, one does not allow the wrath to emerge and represses the emotional feelings deep inside. The hatred which results then becomes like a rope, binding one's heart in a tight knot.

3. RAGE. The Chinese character for "rage" also occurs in the compound "affliction." This emotional reaction is much more severe than hatred. When rage happens, one literally explodes. When things become unbearable, one gets infuriated. Rage is a very fierce emotional reaction.

4. COVERING. This is hiding something inside, keeping it "bottled up" and not allowing it to surface. Basically, one is quite afflicted about something, feeling the kinds of wrath, hatred, and rage described above. But one keeps them to oneself and is not straightforward about expressing those feelings. One does not say, "I can't stand you," "I'm not happy with what you just did," or anything of the sort. One conceals and represses one's feelings, storing them up inside and not letting on to the person directly. But in an indirect way one communicates one's deep-seated negative feelings to the party at whom they are directed, just as violently as if one were to take a knife and try to kill him or her. Or else one may underhandedly find a way to harm the person, "stabbing him or her in the back" by undermining and betraying him or her behind the scenes.

5. DECEIT is a false kindness and phony intention. One appears to be kindly but in fact isn't
really that way. For instance, one may say, "I
have some dope here which I'll give you free.
Here, take some." The person takes the drugs and
thereupon becomes addicted. Having an addiction,
he is then forced to buy dope from the one who
"gave" him the stuff "free" to begin with. That's
an example of deception.

6. FLATTERY. This means playing up to people,
"patting the horse," as it were. It means being
a syncophant, puffing people up, giving them high
hats to wear. For instance one says, "Oh! You've
come here! I was just on my way to see you. I
have a friend who really thinks highly of you. He
is going to want to get together with you and include you in a big business deal he has going,"
and so forth.

Flattery means playing up to those who are
rich when one is poor. Just because someone is
wealthy, one addresses that person with all kinds
of deference, using venerable titles and polite
phrases. "You're quite a fellow, a truly great
man. You are a distinguished person. You're really wonderful." This occurs when ordinary people
are before the President. They scramble for words,
searching for all the nicest things to say and
falling all over themselves to make an impression
in expressing them.

7. CONCEIT. One caught up in this affliction
has a disproportionate sense of one's own worth.
Basically, one doesn't have much sense, but one
thinks more highly of oneself than one does of
others. For example, one may be uneducated and
yet say things like, "What do people with educa-
tions know anyway? What good does it do them? I've
never studied, but look at me--there's good food
on my table and I've got plenty of money in my
pocket." That's being conceited. One feels one's
own value surpasses that of other people.

8. HARMING. This affliction causes one to want
to harm others. One of the Eleven Wholesome Dharmas was Non-harming. This affliction is the exact
opposite of that good dharma.

9. JEALOUSY. This affliction occurs when one
becomes envious of those who surpass one in some
way or other. For example, someone may be endowed
with an excellent memory. Because of this, one

becomes jealous of that person thinking, "If only that person weren't around, then I would be Number One. As long as he's here I don't get to be First." That's jealousy. Or one may get jealous of someone with a higher level of education than one possesses, and end up thinking the same kind of thought: "As long as that person is around, I can't be Number One." Being jealous of anyone who surpasses one in any way is included in the definition of this affliction.

10. STINGINESS. With this affliction, one is tight about one's benefits, not wishing to share them with others. One is unable to give anything away. For instance, if a stingy person has money and it is suggested he part with some of it, he simply can't bring himself to do so. He hangs on to that money, squeezing every penny of it so tightly that it turns to liquid and melts away in his palm. Then he wonders where it went. The pigeons were no doubt stingy in past lives in addition to being greedy. They couldn't give up their possessions so now they must endure the retribution of always having to "sponge" off others. They don't have anything of their own. If you suggested to a pigeon that it give anything away, it would not be able to do it.

Next are the Two Intermediate Afflictions.
11. LACK OF SHAME. One of the Eleven Wholesome Dharmas is "shame," and so this affliction is its opposite. One who lacks shame always feels self-righteous. One assumes one is entitled to do whatever one wishes. One considers oneself a special person, an exceptional individual. Those who call themselves extraordinary simply have no sense of shame. They lack a feeling of repentance.

12. LACK OF REMORSE. One who lacks remorse never really examines whether or not one is up to the standards of others. One never feels that what one does might not be on a par with what others do, nor does one fear ridicule or reprisal. One has no concern for public opinion and feels no sense of embarrassment even when the things one does are in fact mean and lowly. Such a person lacks a feeling of remorse.

Last, we will look at the Eight Major Afflictions. 13. LACK OF FAITH. Among the Eleven Wholesome Dharmas was "faith." This affliction is the exact opposite. One does not believe in anyone.

One does not trust one's teacher or anyone else
either. If the teacher lacks faith, he does not
trust his disciples. If the disciples lack faith,
they do not trust the teacher. A son who lacks
faith will not trust even his father and a father
who lacks faith will not believe his son--much
less need we mention siblings. Brothers and sis-
ters who lack faith will not believe in one another.
Their attitude will be "How can you expect me to
trust you? You should believe in me." When one
gets to the point of thinking that others should
believe in one, always convinced that one is quite
great, then no matter what others tell one, one
will doubt its validity. If one speaks the Dharma
for a person who lacks faith, the reaction will be,
"That's just a bunch of phony words--it's all false.
You call that Dharma? What kind of Dharma, anyway?
You're just trying to trick us." That's the attitude of one who lacks faith. But actually that's
not so far off, for when I speak the Dharma, there
is not a single bit of truth in it. You shouldn't
listen to it. In fact, you should run away really
fast. Be like the person who stayed outside the
door and upon being asked to come in, ran away.
That's an example of a lack of faith.

14. LAZINESS. This affliction is the exact
opposite of vigor. It is being actively non-
vigorous. It is another name for indolence.

15. LAXNESS. Another of the Eleven Wholesome
Dharmas was "non-laxness." This affliction is its
opposite. It means one does not follow the rules
but does whatever one pleases. It's akin to the
"freedom" or "independence" that Americans advocate.
When that concept is carried too far, it results
in laxness. Laxness means not obeying one's par-
ents but proceeding to do exactly what one wants.
This particular affliction is a major reason why
it's such a headache teaching Americans. You
laugh, but it's true.

16. TORPOR. This affliction is what makes one
nod off during the Sutra lectures. In fact, it
doesn't matter what one is doing, as a result of
this affliction, one will fall asleep in the process. Reading a Sutra, one will fall asleep. Bowing to the Buddhas, one will nod off. Listening
to the Sutra lectures, one cannot stay awake.
"Torpor" is different from stupidity. "Stupidity"
is a general darkness and lack of clarity--an

inability to understand what is going on. "Torpor" is a dream-like foggy state of mind in which one is oblivious to what is going on around one. One is sitting there and suddenly everything goes blank. One can't remember anything that has been happening. Listening to Sutras, one suddenly can't remember anything that was just said. It's like being in a dream and yet isn't actually dreaming. It's what's described in the poem:

> If one who is dazed transmits
> the delusion to another,
> When all is said and done,
> neither one understands.
> The teacher falls into the hells,
> And the disciple burrows in
> after him.

17. RESTLESSNESS. With this affliction, one is agitated and can't keep still. One is unable to manage the cultivation of calm, pure states. One runs around aimlessly and chaotically. Sitting, one gets restless and decides to stand. Standing, one gets agitated and decides to sit. Walking, one starts out going north and ends up headed south or starts out east and ends up going west. One is all over the place, unable to settle down. That's what happens to the body.

One's mouth is just as chaotic. Saying whatever one pleases, one "runs off at the mouth" like the demon king who came here the other day full of chaotic and confusing talk.

Restlessness also affects the mind. One does a tremendous amount of uncontrolled thinking. One thought replaces the next in an aimless wandering that goes off on tangents and can't stick to the point. One starts out thinking about one thing and ends up thinking about something entirely different. One's thinking enters "never-never land," and starts to fantasize wildly. "There was a god who told me that in three days I'd get reborn in the heavens. Now did that really happen?" One thinks about things one has no business thinking about. "I went to a certain place in meditation and ended up suspended in empty space. Did that really happen? Or will it happen?" The mind becomes tangled in chaos as one contrives all kinds of non-existent experiences. See how pathetic this affliction is?

18. DISTRACTION. With this affliction one loses proper mindfulness. It's another way to enter "never-never land". But in this case one ends up thinking about things that are not wholesome. Whatever goes against the rules, this person thinks about. But what accords with the rules he doesn't think about. His thinking doesn't accord with the rules when he indulges in this affliction.

19. IMPROPER KNOWLEDGE. With this affliction, one becomes obsessed with defilement. It is all one knows. There is nothing proper at all in one's thinking.

20. SCATTEREDNESS brings about totally wild confusion. The mind becomes mixed-up and divided against itself. This affliction is different from "restlessness."

If we were to go into the subtle details of each one, there is a lot to be said. This will suffice to introduce these Twenty Derivative Afflictions to you. Now that you know about them it's likely that you will give rise to more afflictions, to the point that you will take afflictions as your food and not have to eat. But then that might have its good points. For instance, if there were a famine, then you wouldn't die of hunger because you'd have lots of afflictions to eat.

Text:

VI. THE FOUR UNFIXED are: 1. SLEEP, 2. REGRET, 3. EXAMINATION, and 4. INVESTIGATION.

Commentary:

We have now come to the sixth category of the Fifty-One Dharmas Interactive with the Mind. SIX, THE FOUR UNFIXED. They are known as "unfixed" because they are basically indeterminate. Since there's nothing fixed about them, they are called "unfixed." If there were anything definite about them, they would not be said to be "unfixed." They are indeterminate in that they are not decidedly wholesome or decidedly unwholesome. A decidedly wholesome dharma would be, for example, bringing

forth the Bodhi resolve. A decidedly unwholesome
dharma would be bringing forth defiled dharmas like
thoughts of desire. But unfixed dharmas by nature extend through all states of mind and pervade all locations. They ARE:

THE FOUR UNFIXED DHARMAS

1. Sleep (睡眠) *middha*
2. Regret (恶作) *kaukritya*
3. Investigation (尋)
   vitarka
4. Examination (伺)
   vicara

   1. SLEEP. Sleep is a kind of "dark obscurity"
--a blackness and lack of clarity. But the "lack
of clarity" does not mean inability to understand.
Rather, it refers to a darkness that pervades all
that you do. Sleep can result in two problems.
Externally, it can deprive you of affinities with
other people, and internally it can cause you to
lack wisdom. This "dark lack of clarity" is an
unfixed dharma.
   2. REGRET. Sometimes "regret" is listed first,
and the Chinese characters for regret vary from
list to list, but we will proceed to explain it second. When these dharmas are being explained, you
should pay close attention. Be very attentive and
don't let the explanation of them pass by your
ears like a breeze. I have spoken so many dharmas
for you and afterwards you still don't understand.
When it comes time, you still get angry just the
same. You haven't been able to apply what you've
learned. You continue to pursue whatever you encounter. If that's the case, then there's been no
use at all in listening to this explanation. If
you listen to the Sutras with that attitude, then
even a hundred great aeons of doing so won't be of
any great use. The way it should be is that after
hearing a lecture you think, "The Shastra's telling
me I shouldn't have afflictions, so from now on
I'm not going to give rise to even one of the
Twenty Subsidiary Afflictions and will do away
with the Six Fundamental ones altogether." That's
the way someone who has brought forth the resolve
for Bodhi applies them. It shouldn't be that when
the afflictions are explained, the more names for

them you have, the more of them you give rise to.
That's what I was talking about when I advised you
before that you could now "eat" more afflictions.
Now when you get angry you can wonder if you should
be using "wrath" or "hatred." You did not know
there were so many possibilities before, and now
that you know, it has greatly expanded your functioning. You think, "Let's see, now's a good time
to use 'rage;' or maybe 'covering' is in order.
That way I can take care of you behind your back."
If that's what's happening, then you are making a
big mistake. You've listened to the Shastra in
vain.

"Regret" is also sometimes listed as "doing
it wrong," because it arises with regard to deeds
misdone. "Why did I do that, anyway?" Having done
something wrong, one regrets it. Or one regrets
not having done some bad thing to someone, thinking things like "Why didn't I do such-and-such a
thing to that particular person? That would have
put him in his place for sure. It would have totally done him in. Why didn't I think of it then!"
Or, "Why didn't I slice off his arm with my knife
when I had the chance? That way he couldn't have
hit me." It's that kind of regret that's meant
here. Regret arises when one is not satisfied with
one's actions or inactions or when one feels one
has done something wrong.

3. EXAMINATION, AND 4. INVESTIGATION. "Examination"
is a coarser dharma than "investigation." When
you are just about to act in a way that could be
good or evil, you do a kind of reckoning with yourself. In a sense, you hold a meeting with yourself
and take stock of what you are about to do. You
say to yourself, "If I handle this matter in such-
and-such a way, will it turn out well?" Then you
answer yourself, "No! Don't do that! How could
you?" In this way you have a meeting with yourself. If this "meeting" in your mind is on a
coarse level, then it is called "examination".
This is when you obviously are going back and forth
with yourself. But if your thinking is very subtle
then it's called "investigation". These two unfixed
dharmas are based on discursive thought and it is
by means of discursive thought that the difference
between them is discerned.

Text:

The third is the FORM DHARMAS. In general, there are eleven kinds: I. EYES, II. EARS, III. NOSE, IV. TONGUE, V. BODY, VI. FORMS, VII. SOUNDS, VIII. SMELLS, IX. FLAVORS, X. OBJECTS OF TOUCH, XI. DHARMAS PERTAINING TO FORM.

Commentary:

To review, so far we have discussed:

    I. Eight Mind Dharmas.
    II. Fifty-one Dharmas Interactive
        with the Mind.

And now we come to the third major group:

    III. Eleven Form Dharmas.

    III. THE THIRD IS THE FORM DHARMAS. IN GENERAL, THERE ARE ELEVEN KINDS. "Form Dharmas" refer to those which have shape and substantial physical form--a kind of obstructive quality. They have substantial shape that can be seen and physical form that can be interacted with. They stand in contrast to the mind dharmas and those interactive with the mind.

The Eleven Form Dharmas

1. Eyes (眼) *cakshus*
2. Ears (耳) *shrotra*
3. Nose (鼻) *ghrana*
4. Tongue (舌) *jihva*
5. Body (身) *kaya*
6. Forms (色) *rupa*
7. Sounds (聲) *shabda*
8. Smells (香) *gandha*
9. Flavors (味) *rasa*
10. Objects of Touch (觸)
    sprashtavya
11. Dharmas Pertaining to
    Form (法處所攝色)
    dharmayatanikani rupani

1. EYES. The eyes are classed as a form dharma because not only can they see all kinds of forms, they are themselves physical forms. They have a substantial shape. When the eyes see things that are enjoyable to look at, they never get tired of looking at them. But if they look at things which are unpleasant to see, they object to the sight and resist looking.

2. EARS. The ears hear all kinds of sounds. If the ears hear sounds that are pleasurable, they can listen day after day without any sense of fatigue. But as soon as they hear something that is not pleasant, they don't like it and quickly grow tired of it.

3. NOSE. The nose smells scents and if they are pleasant and fragrant, then the more it smells the better it likes it. It never grows tired of smelling. But if it has to smell some stench, it will object from the moment it gets a whiff of it and grow tired of it immediately.

4. TONGUE. The tongue tastes flavors. If they are pleasant flavors, it is happy to taste them. If the flavors are unpleasant it does not like to taste them. It says, "Ugh, that's too bitter! I don't want to eat it!"

5. BODY. If the body likes something, it wants to get near it and come into contact with it. If it doesn't like something, it wants to stay far away from it.

These are the five "internal" sense organs. The sixth in the list, the faculty of the mind, is not a form dharma, because the intellect belongs to the sixth consciousness, making it a mind dharma.

6. FORMS, 7. SOUNDS, 8. SMELLS, 9. FLAVORS, and 10. OBJECTS OF TOUCH, are all included under the category of Form Dharmas. They are the five "external" sense objects, or "dusts."

11. DHARMAS PERTAINING TO FORM is the eleventh of the Form Dharmas. It is classed as a form dharma because these dharmas are the shadows cast within the intellect of the five external dusts. So even though they happen in the mind, they belong to form.

What is the origin of these Eleven Form Dharmas? It is the nature of the Treasury of the Thus Come One. All these dharmas are composed of the Four Elements.

The Four Elements

1. Earth
2. Air
3. Fire
4. Water

Eyes, ears, nose, tongue, body, forms, sounds, smells, flavors, objects of touch, and dharmas pertaining to form are formed by a combination of the four elements. These sense organs and the sense objects are made from the coming together of the four elements.

Besides that, earth, air, fire, and water fill the entire Dharma Realm. In the *Shurangama Sutra*, the principle of the four elements is discussed in detail and it is shown how they are all the nature of the Treasury of the Thus Come One. Ordinarily we people consider fire and water to be incompatible. However, in the Dharma Realm, water pervades its entirety as does fire. Air and earth also entirely pervade the Dharma Realm. Within the Dharma Realm they assist one another and do not interfere with one another. Water is not incompatible with fire and fire does not hinder water. They all get along just fine! How can this be? It is because in nature they are all the Treasury of the Thus Come One. Our bodies start out as being the four elements and from these arise all the various dharmas. People who have never listened to the Sutras before may find it hard to fathom how our bodies are composed of the four elements, but if you look into it in detail it will become clear to you and you'll know that it's true.

Take for example the moist parts of your body --the perspiration, urine, and all the other liquids. These belong to the element water. Your temperature belongs to the element fire. Your breath belongs to the element air. And your skin, flesh, muscles, and bones belong to the element earth. When the four elements come together in this way, then the eleven Form Dharmas result. This is just a brief explanation of how these Form Dharmas come about. If you really want to know about them, you will have to become enlightened and then you will be able to completely fathom them.

There are only two major categories of dharmas left so my explanation of them will soon be
finished. Then, whether you enter this "door to
understanding" lies with you. Whether I have explained them clearly is my concern. Whether you
have listened to them clearly is your concern. If
you are clear, then you will understand these
Hundred Dharmas. If you are not clear, then you
will not have understood them. If you understand
these Hundred Dharmas, then you will be able to
understand all the essential principles of Buddhism. If you have understood them, then it can
be said you have opened an enlightenment. If you
have not understood them, you can keep studying
them gradually.

Text:

The fourth is the DHARMAS NOT INTERACTIVE
WITH THE MIND. In general, there are twenty-four:
I. ATTAINMENT (AQUISITION), II. LIFE-FACULTY, III.
GENERIC SIMILARITY, IV. DISSIMILARITY, V. THE NO-
THOUGHT SAMADHI, VI. THE SAMADHI OF EXTINCTION,
VII. THE REWARD OF NO THOUGHT, VIII. BODIES OF
NOUNS, IX. BODIES OF SENTENCES, X. BODIES OF PHO-
NEMES, XI. BIRTH, XII. DWELLING, XIII. AGING, XIV.
IMPERMANENCE, XV. REVOLUTION, XVI. DISTINCTION,
XVII. INTERACTION, XVIII. SPEED, XIX. SEQUENCE,
XX. TIME, XXI. DIRECTION, XXII. NUMERATION, XXIII.
COMBINATION, XXIV. DISCONTINUITY.

Commentary:

IV. THE FOURTH IS THE NON-INTERACTIVE ACTIVITY DHARMAS.
"Non-interactive" means not working together with
something else. For example, if there are two of
us and I say, "Let's go east," and you say, "No,
we're going west," then that's called "non-
interactive"--not working together. If we work
together so that when I say "east," you agree and

we both go east, then that's called "interactive." Another example of interaction is when we take some grain in our hands and the pigeons come and eat out of our hands. We have the grain and they want to eat it, so we interact. But if they didn't eat it, then there wouldn't be any interaction.

What is it that these twenty-four dharmas don't interact with? They don't interact with the Mind Dharmas. They don't interact with the Dharmas Interactive with the Mind. They don't interact with the Form Dharmas, and even less would they interact with the Unconditioned Dharmas. That's because they are very special.

Why is it that they don't interact with the Mind or Dharmas Interactive with the Mind? Mind Dharmas and Dharmas Interactive with the Mind are able to climb on conditions. They work on external states. They are conditioned by those outside states. But these dharmas of the Activity Skandha which are not interactive with the other dharmas do not have this ability. They are not conditioned by external states. Therefore, they are not interactive with Mind Dharmas or Dharmas Interactive with the Mind.

You might say that they should then be interactive with the Form Dharmas, but they are not interactive with those either. Why not? If you try to say these dharmas are form dharmas, you must consider the fact that they don't have any substance and they don't have any marks. They have no physical characteristics. All twenty-four of these dharmas are false. They are absolutely and totally false, so don't mistake them for something true. The reason they don't interact with the other dharmas is because they are false and therefore can't combine with anything else at all. Nonetheless they do exist. But although they exist, they have no substance, no shape, no marks, and they do not interact.

In listening to the Dharma you have now learned that dharmas are both true and false. I am describing some false dharmas to you now, but that is because it is necessary for you to know about the false dharmas. If you know about them, then your true nature can appear. But if you don't know about them, how can you obtain your true nature? If you mistake the false for the true, then that becomes the false within the false. That is to be like the Venerable Ananda who wanted to get to the true but was afraid of losing the false. He couldn't give up the false.

> If you can't give up the false,
>   you won't accomplish the true.
> If you can't give up death,
>   you will never exchange it for life.

Why are these twenty-four dharmas not interactive with the Unconditioned Dharmas? It is because although they have no shape or characteristics, they still have production and extinction. For that reason they also are not interactive with the Unconditioned Dharmas, which don't have production and extinction. The reason there is production and extinction involved in these Non-Interactive Activity Dharmas, is because they are basically shadows cast by the Mind Dharmas, the Dharmas Interactive with the Mind, and the Form Dharmas--all acting together. That is also why they are false; why there is actually nothing true in them. Someone's thinking, "Today I wanted to hear some true Dharma but all this Dharma Master has talked about is false dharmas. If I had known his whole lecture was going to be about false dharmas, I wouldn't have come to listen." Well, if you don't listen to false dharmas, then there is no true Dharma. First you have to hear about false dharmas and then you will be able to recognize true Dharma. This is a case of speaking the false for the sake of the true. When you get rid of the false, the true appears.

The Twenty-four
Non-Interactive Activity Dharmas

1. Attainment (得) *prapti*
2. Life Faculty (命根) *jivitendriya*
3. Generic Similarity (衆同分) *nikaya-sabhaga*
4. Dissimilarity (異生性) *visabhaga*
5. No-thought Samadhi (無想定) *asamjnisamapatti*
6. Samadhi of Extinction (滅盡定)
     nirodha-samapatti
7. Reward of No Thought (無想報) *asamjnika*

8. Bodies of Nouns (名身) *namakaya*
9. Bodies of Sentences (句身) *padakaya*
10. Bodies of Phonemes (文身) *vyanjanakaya*
11. Birth (生) *jati*
12. Dwelling (住) *sthiti*
13. Aging (老) *jara*
14. Impermanence (無常) *anityata*
15. Revolution (流轉) *pravritti*
16. Distinction (定異) *pratiniyama*
17. Interaction (相應) *yoga*
18. Speed (勢速) *java*
19. Sequence (次第) *anukrama*
20. Time (時) *kala*
21. Direction (方) *desha*
22. Numeration (數) *samkhya*
23. Combination (和合性) *samagri*
24. Discontinuity (不和合性) *anyathatva*

As to these Non-Interactive Activity Dharmas,
IN GENERAL, THERE ARE TWENTY-FOUR. 1. ATTAINMENT. When
you start out not having something and then you
get it, that is called "attainment." Where does
attainment come from? It arises from greed. Within a state of not wanting anything, you suddenly
want to get something. Now I will show you why
this is a false dharma. Say, for example, you
have a piece of gold. You say, "Oh, I have this
piece of gold. Take a look. It's gold, isn't it?"
But the gold is not "attainment" in itself. Therefore, the concept of "attainment" is just a false
name.
2. LIFE FACULTY. The life faculty, or root of
life, comes from the seeds which reside in the
Eighth Consciousness. When these take on life,
there is the life faculty. When the conditions
of a lifespan, warmth and consciousness are present, there is the life faculty. When the Eighth
Consciousness is in your body, the life faculty
is existent. When the Eighth Consciousness leaves
your body, the life faculty also departs. Therefore, the root of life, the life faculty, is also
false. Don't think, "This life of mine is true.
No matter what, I'm going to take care of this
precious body of mine. Nobody can get away with
bumping into me. I will not allow anyone to say
anything the least bit impolite to me." It's just
because you are unable to give up your root of
life that you are unable to become enlightened.

The life faculty is actually harmful--a detriment
--but you don't realize it. You think it's a
precious treasure. You consider your life to be
valuable and important. But that's just an attachment. You are mistaking the false for the
true. Your self-nature is true but your life is
not true. The life faculty is false.

3. GENERIC SIMILARITY. This refers to factors
which a group shares. For example, you have a
body, which is your share and I have a body which
is mine. The fact that everyone has a body is
then known as a generic similarity. Ordinary people have a generic similarity with other ordinary
people; those of the Two Vehicles have a generic
similarity with others of the Two Vehicles. There's
a generic similarity among Bodhisattvas. However,
within these similarities there are also dissimilarities, which is the next dharma.

4. DISSIMILARITY. Let's take the example of two
people. Because they are people, they have a
generic similarity. But one of these people is
impetuous. He just barges right in and starts
doing things. The other person is cautious. He
hesitates to do anything. Now the impetuous person says of the cautious person, "See that guy?
He doesn't do anything at all. Just eats and
sleeps. What use is he anyway? I think we should
just get rid of people like that."

The cautious person says of the impetuous person, "See that guy? He'll do anything! Anything
at all! It's guys like that who are ruining the
world! I think we should do away with all people
like that!" Basically these are two human beings
but they end up being jealous and obstructive of
each other because of their dissimilarities.

There's another good example of dissimilarities within similarities. Take the armour maker
and the sword smith. They share a similar occupa-
tion--construction of weaponry. But they are on
opposite ends of the spectrum, because the armor
maker is intent upon making a product which will
be invincible against swords, lances, spears,
arrows, and all other kinds of weapons. His aim
is to protect the warrior. The sword smith, on
the other hand, tries to devise weapons which will
pierce the armour. He aims to make his products
so sharp that with a single blow they will rend
the strongest armour. Although both products are

used in the military, one product is for defense
and the other is for offense. That's a dissimilarity within similarity.

Another example is found within Buddhism itself. Basically all Five Schools are similar in
that they are aspects of Buddhism. But when contention arises between members of various schools,
then a dissimilarity occurs within that similarity.
That's why when someone came the other night and
asked me what sect I was, I replied, "I don't have
a sect." If you don't have a sect, then there's
no way anyone can attack you. But if you do have
a sect, then the Ch'an School says that the Teaching School is no good; and the Teaching School
says that the Ch'an School is wrong. They all
slander one another. That's another dissimilarity
within a generic similarity.

Another one occurs among immortals. From time
immemorial the immortals have been getting down
on one another. One will say, "Oh, Confucius--
he's someone who didn't have any sense at all."
Or, one will say, "Mencius? He understood even
less. I have a lot more wisdom than either one
of them." You see? To begin with, they all had
a generic similarity, but when they started slandering one another it ended up creating a dissimilarity.

5. THE NO-THOUGHT SAMADHI. This is a samadhi cultivated by those of externalist ways. What they
do is to suppress production and extinction. They
use a kind of force to prevent the mind and that
which is interactive with the mind from working.
They bring the operation of the mind and the dharmas interactive with the mind to a stop so there
is no actual thinking. But this is really a
forced situation. It's kind of like putting a
heavy rock on some crab grass. You can put the
rock on the grass and press it down so that it
won't grow up, but the roots are still there. So
those in this samadhi are still not free of their
Seventh Consciousness and one of its two innate
attachments.

The Two Innate Attachments
of the Seventh Consciousness

1. The innate attachment to self.
2. The innate attachment to dharmas.

In this samadhi, one is not free of the innate attachment of self.

6. THE SAMADHI OF EXTINCTION. This is another dharma cultivated by those of externalist ways. Again, it is a case of using a kind of force as a means to arrive at extinction. Here, the Sixth Consciousness and the Dharmas Interactive with the Mind cease to function, just as in the No-Thought Samadhi described above. That means that one in this samadhi doesn't strike up false thoughts. Since false thinking is extinguished, it is called the "Samadhi of Extinction." However, the Seventh Consciousness, with its innate attachment to dharmas, has not ceased to function. In the one above it was the innate attachment to self, which is the coarser of the two. Here, the attachment is a bit subtler and is the innate attachment to dharmas. The Seventh Consciousness and the Eighth Consciousness still mingle together and one is not yet free of them. So, although this is called a "samadhi" it is not a true samadhi.

7. THE REWARD OF NO THOUGHT. This is different from the No-Thought Samadhi. The No-Thought Samadhi is a cause. The Reward of No Thought is an effect. The No-Thought Samadhi is a state which can occur when one has not yet given up one's body. It means rebirth in the Heaven of Neither Thought Nor Non-Thought. In this Reward of No-Thought, there remains a very subtle attachment to form which still exists in the Eighth Consciousness and which one takes as one's life. This is referring to an extremely subtle aspect of the Marks Division of the Eighth Consciousness. It causes a person to still feel that he has a life. But this "life" still has an end to it and when that occurs the person can still fall. Remember I talked before about the cultivator who cultivated this Reward of No Thought? When he would sit by the sea in meditation, he was continually disturbed by a fish jumping in the water, until one day he gave rise to hate and got angry. He said, "I'm going to turn into a Kingfisher and get you, fish. I'm going to eat you up." When he relinquished his body, he was born in the Heaven of Neither Thought Nor Non-Thought, obtaining his Reward of No Thought. But after his heavenly blessings were used up, he fell and became reborn as a Kingfisher. That's why when I tell you that

these two pigeons here used to be left-home people who didn't keep the precepts and so this is how they've ended up, you should understand it's the same principle.

8. BODIES OF NOUNS. "Nouns" are the names of people, places, and things. Every human being is called a "person." That's a noun. They also each have their own individual names and those are all nouns. There is also the distinction of general and specific nouns that applies to material objects as well. For example,,we can call this a "burner," or more specifically, an "incense burner." We can call this a "bottle," or more specifically a "flower vase." When a general noun is used, that's just called a noun. When a noun compound is used, that's called a "body of nouns."

9. BODIES OF SENTENCES. Just as Bodies of Nouns are used to delineate dharmas, so too, are "bodies of sentences" used to clarify dharmas.

> All activities are impermanent,
> Characterized by production and
>   extinction.

That is a sentence. When combined with other sentences, it becomes part of a body of sentences. When groups of words are used to reveal dharmas, they are called bodies of sentences.

10. BODIES OF PHONEMES. Phonemes are sounds that carry meaning in a given language. In Chinese, each character has a single sound. When characters are combined in a meaningful way, then one obtains a "body of phonemes." The Sutras are all bodies of phonemes. All kinds of books, articles, treatises, and so forth, are bodies of phonemes.

11. BIRTH, and 12. DWELLING. Everything subject to birth will also dwell. It doesn't matter whether it's people, creatures, or things, they are all subject to 13. AGING, and 14. IMPERMANENCE. "Birth" means that something comes into being which previously did not exist. "Aging" means that although something still exists, it is declining, decaying. Therefore, "aging" is also known as "changing." During the stage of "dwelling" one remains static, but when "aging" begins, things become different. These four refer to the cycle of coming into being, dwelling, decaying, and disappearing.

15. REVOLUTION, 16. DISTINCTION, and 17. INTER-
ACTION also relate to one another. "Revolution"
literally means "turning and flowing," and refers
to how we people have from beginningless time
until the present been turning on the six-path
wheel of rebirth. We have been flowing and turning in birth and death for myriads of kalpas without rest. This process never stops and so it's
called "revolution" on the wheel.

"Distinction" means the "fixing of differen-
ces," and refers, for example, to the distinctions
which occur in the process of cause and effect.
Whatever kind of cause one plants will reap a
corresponding result. But sometimes the same
kinds of causes can lead to different effects.
That aspect of the process is known as "distinction."

"Interaction" is the next dharma. Someone
is wondering how since these twenty-four are
called "Non-Interactive" there can be one among
them called "interaction." That's a good question.
It appears to be a contradiction, but actually it
is not. Basically, these twenty-four dharmas are
non-interactive with the dharmas of the other four
general categories. They do not interact with
the category which follows--Unconditioned Dharmas.
But this dharma of "interaction" does interact
with the dharmas within its own category--the Non-
Interactive Activity Dharmas. The interaction
is that involved with the cycle of cause and effect. The cause is the beginning of the cycle and
the effect is the end result. Between the cause
and the effect there is the Mark of Karma, which
interacts with both the cause and the effect. So
this cycle involves the "revolution," the "distinctions," and the "interactions." The "interaction"
which occurs is decisive--just like a shadow that
follows a shape. It's never off by the least bit.

18. SPEED. This refers to an extremely power-
ful forward momentum. It is found in the flash
of lightning; the velocity of wind; the swiftness
of a bird flying through the air; the quickness of
a rabbit on the run. These are all outward manifestations of speed.

19. SEQUENCE. This dharma is revealed in the
marking of intervals like years, months, days,
hours. The smallest interval of time is a kshana.
The largest is a great kalpa. Time, too, is a dharma.

21. DIRECTION refers to location or placement. We distinguish direction by referring to things as being "in front" or "behind," to the "left" or to the "right," "above" or "below," and so forth in relation to other things.

22. NUMERATION refers to numbering systems.

23. COMBINATION can be blending and uniting, as when milk is mixed with water to form a totality whose parts cannot be distinguished. Or it may be a fitting together, as of a pot with its lid.

24. DISCONTINUITY is the opposite of combination, in that it refers to spontaneity as opposed to causation. Externalists attach to the extreme of spontaneity, whereas those of the Two Vehicles attach to causation--the coming together of causes and conditions. But the nature of the Treasury of the Thus Come One is neither combination nor non-combination. It is neither causes and conditions nor spontaneity--not the discontinuity or the combination of these two dharmas here.

Text:

The fifth is the UNCONDITIONED DHARMAS, of which there are, in general, six: I. UNCONDITIONED EMPTY SPACE, II. UNCONDITIONED EXTINCTION WHICH IS ATTAINED BY SELECTION, III. UNCONDITIONED EXTINCTION WHICH IS UNSELECTED, IV. UNCONDITIONED UNMOVING EXTINCTION, V. UNCONDITIONED EXTINCTION OF FEELING AND THINKING, VI. UNCONDITIONED TRUE SUCHNESS.

Commentary:

V. THE FIFTH IS THE UNCONDITIONED DHARMAS OF WHICH THERE ARE, IN GENERAL, SIX.

The Six Unconditioned Dharmas

1. Unconditioned Empty Space (虛空無為) *akasha*
2. Unconditioned Extinction Which is Attained Through Selection (擇滅無為) *pratisamkhyanirodha*

3. Unconditioned Extinction which is
   Unselected (非擇滅無為) *apratisamkhyanirodha*
4. Unconditioned Unmoving Extinction
   (不動滅無為) *aninjya*
5. Unconditioned Extinction of Feeling
   and Thinking (想受滅無為)
   samjnavedayitanirodha
6. Unconditioned True Suchness (真如無為)
   Tathata

1. UNCONDITIONED EMPTY SPACE. Empty space is basically unconditioned, so there is no need to
describe it as unconditioned. But here the "unconditioned" refers to one's ability to contemplate empty space as unconditioned. It means to
be able to "illumine and view the Five Skandhas
all as empty." Then there is no mark of self, no
mark of others, no mark of living beings, and no
mark of a lifespan.
   You may say, "Well, I cultivate and have a
little skill. I always sleep sitting up and never
lie down. I only eat one meal a day." But if you
still know that you sleep sitting up and never lie
down then you still haven't reached Unconditioned
Empty Space. If you still know that you eat only
one meal a day then you still haven't reached Unconditioned Empty Space. If you know that you
cultivate, then you haven't reached Unconditioned
Empty Space. Because Unconditioned Empty Space
means that your self-nature is like empty space;
your body is like empty space; what you contemplate
and cultivate is like empty space--devoid of a
mark of self, a mark of others, a mark of living
beings, and a mark of a lifespan. When you reach
that state, then when someone punches you, it's
as though they were punching empty space. Just
think what it would be like to punch empty space.
Empty space wouldn't put up any opposition at all.
Empty space certainly wouldn't hit you back. If
you can cultivate so that you get to be like empty
space, then nothing will be able to bother you.
That is the meaning of Unconditioned Empty Space.
   Unconditioned Empty Space is extremely wonderful. I always tell you this, but you never think it
is very interesting because you hear it every day.
What is it? It's just, "everything's okay." If you
can really have it be that "everything's okay,"

then you are like empty space, because empty
space contains everything within it. Can you
think of anything that is not in empty space?
And there is nothing that empty space rejects.
It never gets upset with you and says, "You, there,
who are part of my empty space. You got it so
dirty! How can you have gone to the toilet there
and gotten my empty space so dirty?" It doesn't
think that way. Pigeons, too, for their part are always up in empty space flying around, and empty
space doesn't get in the way at all.

If we were to really discuss Unconditioned
Empty Space in detail, there would be a lot to say.
But you should always contemplate empty space and
then you'll get so that you have no mark of self,
no mark of others, no mark of living beings, and
no mark of a lifespan. Then you will unite with
everything.

> Unite your virtue with heaven and earth.
> Unite your light with the sun and moon.
> Unite your order with that of the
>   four seasons.
> Unite your good and bad luck with the
>   ghosts and spirits.

When you are like that, then however great the
virtuous nature of heaven is, your virtuous nature
is just that great. However great the virtuous
nature of earth is, your virtuous nature is just
as great. The light of the sun is really bright,
but your light is just as bright as the sun's.
The moon is also bright, but your light is as
bright as the light of the moon. That's what's
meant by uniting your light with the sun and moon.

Spring, summer, fall, and winter are the four
seasons. If you cultivate so that you are just
like empty space, then when springtime comes, you
have the same kind of representation of spring
come to you. In the same way, you represent all
the four seasons as they occur. In the spring
the myriad things come into being. In the summer
the myriad things increase and grow. In the fall
the myriad things are harvested, and in the winter
they are stored away. You can unite your order
with that of the four seasons.

You can also know what the ghosts and spirits
know. Take a look at that! Would you say that is

wonderful or not? When you are about to reach Unconditioned Empty Space, then you become one with
the natural order of things.

2. UNCONDITIONED EXTINCTION WHICH IS ATTAINED BY
SELECTION. "Selection" means choosing. But you
say, "If it's selected, it seems to me it would
be conditioned, wouldn't it?" Yes, the "selection" is conditioned, but at the time when the
"extinction" is reached, then it is unconditioned.
That is why this dharma is not considered to be
a conditioned dharma. The first ninety-four
dharmas were all conditioned. It's only these
six which are unconditioned. When one reaches
"extinction which is attained by selection" one
has no body, so that can be considered unconditioned.

3. UNCONDITIONED EXTINCTION WHICH IS UNSELECTED.
That is when, without making use of the power to
choose or select, one's basic nature is pure. The
previous dharma, Unconditioned Extinction Which
is Attained by Selection, is the kind of Nirvana
certified to by Bodhisattvas of Provisional Enlightenment. Also, when those of the Two Vehicles
discriminate marks and contemplate emptiness, by
dividing form into its separate characteristics
and further dividing and dividing until all marks
disappear and form becomes emptied, this, too, is
known as "Unconditioned Extinction Which is Attained by Selection." Now this dharma, Unconditioned Extinction Which is Unselected, refers to
the original purity of one's self-nature. This
is the state certified to by Bodhisattvas of
Actual Enlightenment.

Bodhisattvas of Provisional Enlightenment
sever one portion of ignorance in order to certify
to one portion of enlightenment. The Enlightenment they certify to is directly proportionate to
the amount of ignorance they cut off. That's Unconditioned Extinction Which is Attained by Selection.

Unconditioned Extinction Which is Unselected
is subdivided into two categories:

The Two Divisions of
Unconditioned Extinction Which is Unselected

1. Absence of Conditioning Factors
2. Original Purity of the Self-Nature

With the first kind, the required factors
for conditioning are not present. This state of
Unconditioned Extinction Which is Unselected can
sometimes be experienced by ordinary people or
those of the Two Vehicles. The other kind is that
to which Bodhisattvas of Actual Enlightenment certify.

4. UNCONDITIONED UNMOVING EXTINCTION. "Unmoving"
refers to cultivation of samadhi of not moving.
This kind of unmovingness is original and basic
stillness. It is not the kind of "non-movement"
attained in the No-Thought Samadhi. Therefore,
this is an unconditioned dharma.

5. UNCONDITIONED EXTINCTION OF FEELING AND THINKING.
With the previous Unconditioned Dharma of Unmoving
Extinction, one is reborn in the Heavens of the
Form Realm. With the attainment of Unconditioned
Extinction of Feeling and Thinking, one is reborn
in the Formless Realm. When one attains this
dharma, one's mind is not moved by suffering or
by pleasure. There is no concept   of what's
meant by "suffering" or what's meant by "pleasure."
One is not shaken by either of these states. It's
not like we people who upon encountering a state
of suffering can't stand it and upon encountering
a state of pleasure want to pursue it. For example, you hear someone say, "Ah! Here's something
that doesn't exist in this country. You should
try it out. It's really good to eat!" You say,
"Really! I'll try some!" and you go running after
flavor. You see how pleasure and pain have moved
your mind? But when one is certified to this kind
of unconditioned extinction of feeling and thinking, pleasure and pain no longer move one's mind.
You can experience pleasure and endure pain without any kind of effort on your part. You don't
have to use patience to do it. You just basically
don't move in the midst of it. This again is
basically "everything's okay." When you think,
what do you think of? When you feel, what do you
feel? You think about and feel pleasure and pain.
But when these don't move your mind, then you
have certified to the Unconditioned Extinction of
Feeling and Thinking. Are there any of you who
cultivate the Way who have managed to cultivate
to this state? If you get to this state you can
go to the Heavens of the Formless Realm, specifically, the Five Heavens of No Return, which are

where Arhats of the Third Fruition abide.

When you've cultivated to the point that you don't feel pain or pleasure, then you don't "accept" anything. That is like Shariputra's Uncle who held the doctrine of "non-acceptance." His intention was to not accept pleasure or pain and this was supposed to indicate that he had a lot of samadhi-power. But when the Buddha asked, "Well, do you accept your own view on this?" Shariputra's uncle was stuck. He couldn't come up with an answer, because basically his doctrine of non-acceptance was itself a viewpoint. If he wasn't accepting views, then basically he couldn't accept his own doctrine. By asking one simple question, the Buddha made it so his doctrine could not stand. That's because the Uncle still hadn't reached the state of "everything's okay." He still held this doctrine of non-acceptance, and thereby was defeated. If he could have been without acceptance or non-acceptance then there also would have been no victory or defeat.

5. UNCONDITIONED TRUE SUCHNESS. What is "True Suchness?" You say, "I've heard this explained before. It's one's basic Buddha Nature which is also called Nirvana and also known as the Treasury of the Thus Come One. It has many names. That's 'True Suchness' isn't it?"

Yes, it is. But you still don't recognize what that is. And if it weren't that, you would recognize it even less. What's "that"? It is non-falseness and non-inversion. Being non-false and non-inverted is being "Thus, Thus, unmoving; clear, clear and constantly bright."

In order to know True Suchness, we must first know about the Three Natures.

The Three Natures

1. The Nature Pervasively Calculated and Attached To.
2. The Nature That Arises Dependent on Something Else.
3. The Perfectly Accomplished Real Nature.

We living beings have these first two kinds of inversion, whereas True Suchness is the Perfectly Accomplished Real Nature.

Suppose you were walking at night and you

thought you had spotted a huge snake on the road
ahead. You might let out a yell, "Wow! That's a
really long snake! It's several feet long! How
horrible!" Seeing a snake in the distance like
that is the Nature Pervasively Calculated and Attached To, and leads to your being terrified and
deciding, "Oh! A snake! I've got to get out of
here right away!" So you go running back down the
road and you overtake a person who had earlier passed the same spot you were approaching when you
saw the snake--the Nature Pervasively Calculated
and Attached To.

The person asks you, "Why are you running?"
"You just came along that road. Didn't you
see the big snake back there?" you reply.
"Where?" says the other fellow. "Why don't
we go back and see where it is and we can beat it
to death." So the two of you go back, but when
you get there it's no longer a snake. It's turned
into something else--a piece of rope on the road.
That it's not a snake is the Nature That Arises
Dependent on Something Else. Considering it to be
a snake to start with was the Nature Pervasively
Calculated and Attached To. Now it becomes the
Nature That Arises Dependent on Something Else--
basically it's a piece of rope. So the Nature Pervasively Calculated and Attached To was false--
imaginary. However, the Nature That Arises Dependent on Something Else also turns out to be a dis-
tortion, for in fact the rope itself is made out
of hemp. That it's made from hemp is the Perfectly
Accomplished Real Nature. What started out as
hemp could turn into a piece of rope and then could
turn into a snake. Who would you say caused it to
transform?

The Perfectly Accomplished Real Nature stands
for True Suchness. True Suchness is non-false and
non-distorted, not inverted. That's what is meant
when it is said:

> People who have perfected their culti-
> vation have already ended all falseness
> and have already exhausted all inversion,
> so they are not upside-down.

That's the Perfectly Accomplished Real Nature, also
known as True Suchness. But this "True Suchness"
is still not *real* True Suchness, but false: for if

you *know* it, it still can't be called real. Real
True Suchness is that basically there isn't any
True Suchness. Real True Suchness is nothing at
all. There's no sameness and no difference. There
are no dharmas and no non-dharmas. This is the
basic substance of every single dharma, just as
water has waves but the waves are not the water.
The basic substance of water is water. True Suchness is the basic substance of all dharmas. If
it were not for True Suchness, then dharmas would
not have a basic substance. It's like the rope.
The rope's basic substance is hemp. True Suchness
is not just one, and yet it is not dual. It is
not dharmas and it is not non-dharmas. It's not
identical and not different, not dharmas and not
non-dharmas. That's real True Suchness, the sixth
unconditioned dharma.

Text:

What is meant by there being no self? There
are, in general, Two Kinds of Non-self: 1. the
Non-self of Pudgala, and 2. the Non-self of
Dharmas.

Commentary:

WHAT IS MEANT BY THERE BEING NO SELF? Someone
says, "What do you mean 'no self'? I'm right
here. I'm truly and actually here, so how can you
say there's no me? Aren't you just trying to
cheat us?" That way of thinking is just a case
of not understanding dharmas. If you did understand the Hundred Dharmas, then you would know
that there's got to be no self.
THERE ARE, IN GENERAL, TWO KINDS OF NON-SELF: 1. THE
NON-SELF OF PUDGALA.

The Two Kinds of Non-Self

1. The Non-self of *Pudgala* (no me or mine)
2. The Non-self of Dharmas (no *svabhava* --
    inherent nature)

"Pudgala" is a Sanskrit word which translates as "multiple graspings at destinies." This

refers to numerous comings and goings--turning
around in the Six Destinies.

The Six Destinies

Three Good Paths	Three Evil Paths
1. gods	4. animals
2. asuras	5. ghosts
3. people	6. hell-beings

All ordinary people and all creatures just
keep turning around and around on the revolving
wheel of the Six Paths. These are also known as
the Six Ordinary Dharma Realms.

The Four Sagely Dharma Realms

1. Buddhas
2. Bodhisattvas
3. Those Enlightened to Conditions
4. Sound Hearers

Altogether these make Ten Dharma Realms. Where
do these ten come from? They are all just the
manifestation of a single thought of yours or mine.
If your mind thinks of cultivating and becoming
a Buddha, then in the future you will be able to
become a Buddha. Your thinking of doing this
makes it happen. If you think about cultivating
to become a Bodhisattva, in the future you will
be able to become a Bodhisattva. If your mind
thinks about becoming a person of the Two Vehicles
--a Sound Hearer or One Enlightened to Conditions
--then you will become one or the other. If your
mind thinks about ascending to the heavens, in
the future you can be born in the heavens. All
you need do is hold the Five Precepts and practice the Ten Good Acts and you will gain rebirth
in the heavens. If you say, "Well, I want to be
a person," then just offer up all good conduct
and don't do any evil and you can be a person. If
you are thinking of becoming an asura, then get
angry all the time and think about killing people.
If you do that, then that in itself is the Dharma
Realm of the asuras and in the future you will
become an asura. Those are the Three Good Paths.
Then there are the Three Evil Paths. If you

are greedy all the time--if you have tremendous
greed--then you can fall into the hells. If your
hatred is heavy, if you keep getting angry from
morning to night, you can turn into a hungry ghost.
If you are extremely stupid, then you will end up
as an animal. So if you have greed, anger, and
stupidity you will fall into the evil paths. If
you cultivate precepts, samadhi, and wisdom, then
you'll be born into the Three Good Paths and will
have the possibility of becoming a Buddha in the
future.

Turning in the Six Paths is dangerous business. There's an old saying about it:

> Out of the horse's belly
> Into the womb of a cow.
> How many times have you passed
> Back and forth through Yama's
>   halls?
> First you go for a swing by
>   Shakra's Palace,
> And then plummet back down
>   into Sir Yama's pot.

One just finishes a rebirth as a horse and
ends up back in the womb of a cow. How many times
have you done that? Too many. You're so familiar
with that route by Yama's door that you could walk
it with your eyes closed. You don't know how many
times you've done it. You may make it up to the
Jade Emperor's heavenly halls for a time, but once
again you fall into the pot of boiling oil that
King Yama always has hot. When you become a person, that is made from your mind. When you become
an animal, that also comes about from your mind.
If you act like an animal, in the future you will
become an animal. If you act like a person, in
the future you will be a person. If you act like
a ghost, in the future you will be a ghost.

Some people say they don't believe in ghosts.
Why do they say that? It's because they themselves
are ghosts and they are afraid others will recognize them as such. So they are always telling
others not to believe there are such things as
ghosts. I often say, "Basically there's no real
difference between Buddhas and ghosts. If you are
evil to the ultimate point, then you're a ghost.
If you are good to the ultimate point, then you're

a Buddha. If you cultivate to the point of becoming enlightened, then you're a Buddha. If you
don't get enlightened and keep being stupid, then
you're a ghost. Basically there's no difference.

Some people believe in the Buddha and say,
"Buddhas exist." But they don't believe that there
are ghosts. They say, "There aren't any ghosts."
Why do they say this is so? "I haven't seen any
ghosts," they argue, "so I don't believe any such
things exist."

I ask them, "Well have you seen Buddhas?" I
can safely ask them that because if they haven't
seen ghosts, then they haven't seen Buddhas. So
I say to them,"You have never seen Buddhas either,
so why do you believe in them? If you haven't
seen them, you shouldn't believe in them either,
right?"

They say, "I have seen Buddha images." Well
there are pictures of ghosts around, too. If you
see Buddha images and therefore believe in Buddhas,
then when you see pictures of ghosts, shouldn't
you believe in ghosts? It's strange: such people
are more stupid than animals. I'll tell you
right now that those who don't believe in ghosts
are this way because they don't have the wisdom
to believe ghosts exist. They don't have the true
and actual, perfectly fused and unobstructed wisdom to know this principle. "If you don't believe
in ghosts, you shouldn't believe in the Buddha,
either. There just won't be anything at all. How
will that be?" Of course, originally there isn't
anything at all. Basically there's no self and
also no people, no Buddhas, no ghosts, nothing at
all. But you have to reach that state. You must
truly have achieved   the level of no self. It
can't be that when talking there's no self but
when the time comes to eat you eat more than anyone else. There's a self in that. Or when it
comes time to work you say, "But I heard the Dharma
Master say to be without self, so 'I' shouldn't
do any work." But when the time comes to eat, his
self is suddenly in existence again, because he
definitely has to eat. You have to genuinely be
without a self. That means there aren't any attachments. If you are attached to the existence
of a self then you have an Attachment to Self and
that presents causes and conditions which obstruct
the Way.

Even if you have no self, you still need to be without dharmas. Dharmas must also disappear. Dharmas are used for the sake of the self, so if there's no self, what do you need dharmas for? Then dharmas have no use, either. If you don't have a self, then you have broken your attachment to self, which is also the Obstacle of Afflictions. If you get rid of dharmas, then you've broken through the attachment to dharmas and you've also broken through the Obstacle of the Known. When you have not broken through your attachment to dharmas, then this is how the Obstacle of the Known manifests. You say things like "Take a look at me! See? I understand all six hundred rolls of the Prajna Sutras. I've read them I don't know how many times. I can lecture the *Dharma Flower Sutra* and explain the *Shurangama Sutra*." And so you have the Obstacle of the Known. Whatever it is, you know about it. In this way you produce an obstacle, the obstacle being, "I know and you don't know. I can lecture and you can't lecture. I can cultivate and you can't cultivate. I have all kinds of Way virtue and you don't have any Way virtue. I have wisdom and you don't have wisdom." If dharmas were also empty, then you would not have this obstacle, but would certify to the second kind of non-self.

2. THE NON-SELF OF DHARMAS. Then, although you understand dharmas, it's just as if you didn't. "What in the world is the use of studying Dharma, anyway, then?" you may conclude. Well, if you can know and yet not know, then that's really knowing. That's real wisdom. Then you have broken through the Obstacle of the Known and the Obstacle of Afflictions.

The Two Obstacles

1. The Obstacle of Afflictions
2. The Obstacle of the Known

The Obstacle of Afflictions. Why do you have afflictions? They come from your attachment to self. If you didn't have a self, where would you go to find afflictions? Therefore, the Non-self of the *pudgala* smashes the Obstacle of Afflictions.

The Obstacle of the Known. The Non-self of Dharmas smashes the Obstacle of the Known.

So this passage discusses the Non-self of the
Pudgala and the Non-self of Dharmas to explain the
last part of the Buddha's quote which began the
Shastra:

As the World Honored One has said,
all dharmas have no self.

So it can't be that you simply break through the
attachment to self and yet harbor an attachment
to how well you comprehend dharmas. You have to
also renounce the thought of understanding dharmas. This absence of self refers to one's view
of self, not to the physical body. One should be
devoid of a view of self and a view of dharmas.

All ordinary people are attached to the existence of a self. Those who manage to not be attached to a self become attached to dharmas. The
Buddha knew what was in the minds of living beings
and he wanted to break through their Obstacles of
Afflictions and their Obstacles of the Known. He
spoke all kinds of Dharmas for the purpose of
smashing these obstacles. However, it's really
easy to talk about having no view of self. When
a person gets to the point of not having a self,
he thinks, "Hey! Look at me! I don't have a
self!" So who's talking about not having a self?
Who's that? Or else he speaks the Dharma coming
and going and says, "I speak Dharma better than
anybody! But it's not me speaking, it's the Bodhisattvas speaking," in a roundabout way ascribing
to himself a Bodhisattva position. Then, sitting
upon that Bodhisattva pedestal he has fashioned for
himself, he still has a self. So you see, it's not
easy. It's not something that can be brought
about merely by making that claim. You can't just
say, "I have no self" for it to be the case. Your
"no self" still harbors a self within it. So in
discussing dharmas you need to understand them in
a fundamental way. It can't be that you seem to
understand them but really don't. Anyone with any
knowledge will catch on to that very quickly,
and know that you are simply a person who's fond
of wearing high hats. Your view of self is still
not empty.

Now let us investigate the self. The head
is called a "head." The hair is called "hair."
The eyes are called "eyes." The ears are called

"ears." The nose is called a "nose." And it goes on like this down through the hands being called "hands" and the feet being called "feet" and the fingernails being called "fingernails," to the eighty-four thousand hair pores being called "hair pores." The three hundred and sixty bones are called "bones" and in addition each has it's own individual name. But if you search throughout your entire body, from the top of your head to the soles of your feet, where can you find a "self"? What location can be given the name "self"? What bit of flesh has that name? What drop of blood is known as the "self"? Keep searching for the location of that "self" and you will find that in the entire body there's not a single place that can be called "self". So why are you still attached to a self"?

You say, "I know where I am." If you really know, then that's all right; however, it may be that you don't have a pure concept in mind. You don't really purely know and that's a kind of defiled dharma. But do you recognize your true, actual, pure self--your basic self-nature? Do you ultimately know where that is? Well, look for it. See if you can find it.

I am here lecturing and I have a self. You are there listening with your "selves". So you wonder, "If I don't listen to the Sutras, does that mean I have no self?" No. If you don't listen to the Sutras it just means your "self" is not here listening to Sutras, but it does not mean that your "self" does not exist. But if you could listen to the Sutras as if you were not here, then you'd have gotten a little bit of skill.

"Right!" someone thinks, "I've got that kind of skill because just now I was thinking about going to a bar to get some wine and I was not really 'here' at all."

No. That's not being "here," because you're false thinking. That's just allowing your mind to wander--running off. The way it should be is that there's "no going out and no coming in." You neither run off nor are you here. That is what we're talking about. If you're that way, then that's pretty much "it". What's "it"? It's nonself.

Now I've finished lecturing the Shastra, and you can just consider it as if I hadn't said a

thing, because there should be no self. I didn't
lecture and you didn't listen--everyone is devoid
of self. The non-self is the true, real, and
wonderful self. Someone's thinking, "This Dharma
Master just tells stories."

I learned from you. I don't know who you
learned it from.

END

Index

Index of Sanskrit Terms

THE BUDDHIST TEXT TRANSLATION SOCIETY

CHAIRPERSON: The Venerable Tripitaka Master Hsüan Hua
-Abbot of Gold Mountain Monastery, Gold
Wheel Monastery, and Tathagata Monastery
-Chancellor of Dharma Realm Buddhist
University
-Professor of the Tripitaka and the Dhyanas

PRIMARY TRANSLATION COMMITTEE:

Chairpersons: Venerable Tripitaka Master Hsüan Hua
Bhikshuni Heng Ch'ih

Members:

Bhikshu Heng Sure
Bhikshu Heng Kuan
Bhikshu Heng Shun
Bhikshu Heng Ch'au
Bhikshu Heng Tso
Bhikshu Heng Ch'i
Bhikshu Heng Gung
Bhikshu Heng Wu
Bhikshu Heng Jau
Bhikshu Heng Ch'ang

Bhikshuni Heng Ch'ing
Bhikshuni Heng Chü
Bhikshuni Heng Chai
Bhikshuni Heng Wen

Bhikshuni Heng Tao
Bhikshuni Heng Ming
Bhikshuni Heng Hsien
Bhikshuni Heng Jieh
Bhikshuni Heng Tsai
Bhikshuni Heng Duan
Bhikshuni Heng Bin
Bhikshuni Heng Liang
Bhikshuni Heng Lyan
Bhikshuni Heng Chia
Upasika Terri Nicholson
Upasaka David Rounds
Upasaka R.B. Epstein
Upasaka Chou Li-jen

REVIEWING COMMITTEE:

Chairpersons: Bhikshu Heng Tso
Upasaka Kuo Jung Epstein

Members:

Bhikshu Heng Sure
Bhikshu Heng Kuan
Bhikshu Heng Gung
Bhikshu Heng Wu
Bhikshuni Heng Ch'ih
Bhikshuni Heng Chai
Bhikshuni Heng Wen
Bhikshuni Heng Tao

Bhikshuni Heng Hsien
Bhikshuni Heng Tsai
Bhikshuni Heng Duan
Bhikshuni Heng Bin
Bhikshuni Heng Liang
Upasika Hsien Ping-ying
Upasaka David Rounds
Upasaka Chou Li-jen

Publications from the
Buddhist Text Translation Society

All BTTS translations include extensive inter-linear commentary by the Venerable Tripitaka Master Hsuan Hua, unless otherwise noted. All works available in
softcover only unless otherwise noted.
ISBN Prefix: 0-917512

SUTRAS (Scriptures spoken by the Buddha):

AMITABHA SUTRA - Explains the causes and circumstances
for rebirth in the Land of Ultimate Bliss of Amitabha
Buddha. 01-4, 204 pgs., $8.00. (Also available in
Spanish. $8.00)

BRAHMA NET SUTRA - Vol. I contains the Ten Major Precepts,
and the first Twenty Minor Precepts. English/Chinese.
79-0, 300 pgs., $10.00.
  Vol. II - The Twenty-first Minor Precept through the
  Forty-Eighth Minor Precept. English/Chinese. 88-X,
  210 pgs., $8.00.
  Entire text only is also available. 56-1, $5.00.

DHARANI SUTRA - Tells of the past events in the life of
the Bodhisattva of Great Compassion, Avalokiteshvara
(Kuan Yin). It explains the meaning of the mantra line
by line, and contains Chinese poems and drawings of division bodies of Kuan Yin for each of the 84 lines of the
mantra. Drawings and verses on each of the 42 Hands and
Eyes of Kuan Yin. 13-8, 352 pgs., $12.00.

千手千眼大悲心陀羅尼經 - DHARANI SUTRA - Original
Chinese text only. 210 pgs., $6.00.

DHARMA FLOWER (LOTUS)SUTRA- This Sutra, spoken in the
last period of the Buddha's teaching, proclaims the ulti-
mate principles of the Dharma which unites all previous
teachings into one. The following are volumes which
have been published to date:
  VOL. I   INTRODUCTION.
  VOL. II INTRODUCTION, CHAPTER ONE.
  VOL. III EXPEDIENT METHODS, CHAPTER TWO.
  VOL. IV A PARABLE, CHAPTER THREE.
  VOL. V   BELIEF AND UNDERSTANDING, CHAPTER FOUR.
  VOL. VI MEDICINAL HERBS, CHAPTER FIVE, and CON-
  FERRING PREDICTIONS, CHAPTER SIX.
  VOL. VII PARABLE OF THE TRANSFORMATION CITY,
  CHAPTER SEVEN.
  VOL. VIII FIVE HUNDRED DISCIPLES RECEIVE PRE-
  DICTIONS, CHAPTER EIGHT, and BESTOWING PREDIC-
  TIONS UPON THOSE STUDYING AND BEYOND STUDY,
  CHAPTER NINE.
  VOL. IX THE DHARMA MASTER, CHAPTER TEN, and
  VISION OF THE JEWELED STUPA, CHAPTER II.

VOL. X DEVADATTA, CHAPTER TWELVE. Coming Soon.

FLOWER ADORNMENT (AVATAMSAKA) SUTRA VERSE PREFACE
清涼國師 華嚴經序淺釋); a succinct verse commentary by T'ang
Dynasty National Master Ch'ing Liang (the Master of seven
emperors), which gives a complete overview of all the fundamental principles contained in the Sutra in eloquent
style. First English translation. BI-LINGUAL EDITION
Chinese and English. 244 pgs., 28-6, $7.00.

FLOWER ADORNMENT SUTRA PROLOGUE. A detailed explanation
of the principles of the Sutra utilizing the Hsien Shou
method of analyzing scriptures known as the Ten Doors,
by National Master Ch'ing Liang. The following volumes
have been published to date:

> VOL. I, THE FIRST DOOR: THE CAUSES AND CONDITIONS
> FOR THE ARISAL OF THE TEACHING. 252 pgs., p.66-9
> $10.00.
> VOL. II, THE SECOND DOOR: THE STORES AND TEACHINGS
> TO WHICH IT BELONGS. PART ONE. 280 pgs., 73-1,
> $10.00.

清涼國師 華嚴經疏淺釋 entirety of the AVATAMSAKA SUTRA
PROLOGUE, from First to Tenth Door, together with inter-
linear commentary by Ven. Abbot Hua, in four Volumes.
CHINESE $5.00, $8.50, $8.50, and $5.00.

FLOWER ADORNMENT SUTRA - Known as the king of kings of
all Buddhist scriptures because of its great length,
(81 rolls containing more than 700,000 Chinese characters), and its profundity; it contains the most complete
explanation of the Buddha's state and the Bodhisattva's
quest for Awakening. When completed, the entire Sutra
text with commentary is estimated to be from 75 to 100
volumes. The following volumes have been published to
date:

> FLOWER STORE SEA OF ADORNED WORLDS, CHAPTER 5,
> PART I. Available Soon.
> BRIGHT ENLIGHTENMENT, CHAPTER 9. Available Soon.
> PURE CONDUCT, CHAPTER 11. Available Soon.
> TEN DWELLINGS, CHAPTER 15. 77-4, 185 pgs., $8.00.
> BRAHMA CONDUCT, CHAPTER 16. 80-4, 65 pgs., $4.00.
> THE MERIT AND VIRTUE FROM FIRST BRINGING FORTH
> THE MIND, CHAPTER 17. 83-9, 200 pgs., $7.00.
> TEN INEXHAUSTIBLE TREASURIES, CHAPTER 22. 38-3,
> 184 pgs., $7.00.
> PRAISES IN THE TUSHITA HEAVEN PALACE, CHAPTER 24.
> 39-1.
> TEN TRANSFERENCES, CHAPTER 25, PART I. Available Soon.
> TEN GROUNDS, CHAPTER 26, PART I. 87-1, 234 pgs, $7.00.
> TEN GROUNDS, CHAPTER 26, PART II. 74-X, 200 pgs.,
> $8.00.

華嚴經十地品淺釋 The Second to the Tenth Grounds,
contains the Bodhisattva's successive certification to
each of the Sagely Grounds. CHINESE only. Grounds Two
to Five in one volume now available; remaining Grounds
forthcoming.

ENTERING THE DHARMA REALM, CHAPTER 39. This chapter
relates the spiritual journey of the Youth Good Wealth
in his search for Ultimate Awakening. In his quest he
meets fifty-three "Good Teachers," each of whom represents a successive stage on the Bodhisattva path. The
following volumes have been published to date:

PART 1. Describes the setting for the Youth's quest, and his meeting with Manjushri Bodhisattva. 280 pgs., 68-5, $8.50.

PART 2. Good Wealth meets his first ten teachers, who represent the positions of the Ten Dwellings. 250 pgs., 73-1, $8.50.

PART 3. The ten teachers who correspond to the levels of the Ten Conducts. 250 pgs., 73-1, $8.50.

PART 4. The ten teachers who represent the First to Sixth Grounds. 300 pgs., 81-2, $9.00.

PART 5. The four teachers who represent the Seventh to Tenth Grounds of a Bodhisattva. Available December, 1982.

HEART SUTRA AND VERSES WITHOUT A STAND - The text explains the meaning of Prajna Paramita, the perfection of wisdom. Each line in the Sutra is accompanied by an eloquent verse by the Ven. Abbot Hua. 160 pgs., 28-7, $7.50.

般若波羅蜜多心經非台頌解 same as above, including the commentary. IN CHINESE. 120 pgs., $5.00.

SHURANGAMA SUTRA This Sutra, which reveals the Shurangama Samadhi and which contains the Shurangama Mantra, primarily concerns the mind.

VOL. 1. Seven locations of the mind are all refuted. 289 pgs., 17-0, $8.50.

VOL. II. Ten aspects of seeing; individual and collective karma. 212 pgs., 25-1, $8.50.

VOL. III. Six sense organs, objects and consciousnesses and seven elements. 240 pgs., 94-4, $8.50.

VOL. IV. Continuity of world, living beings and karmic retribution. 200 pgs., 90-1, $8.50.

VOL. V. Twenty-five sages tell of their perfect penetration. Kuan Yin Bodhisattva's method is selected by Manjushri Bodhisattva as most appropriate for people in this world. 250 pgs., 91-X, $8.50.

SHRAMANERA VINAYA AND RULES OF DEPORTMENT - This text, by Great Master Lien Ch'ih of the Ming Dynasty, explains the moral code for Shramaneras (novice monks). 112 pgs., 04-9, $4.00.

緇門崇行錄 An ancient text compiled by Great Master Lien Ch'ih of the Ming Dynasty, on the Vinaya (moral code) for Bhikshus. No commentary. CHINESE. 130 pgs.

SHURANGAMA MANTRA COMMENTARY -Explains how to practice the foremost mantra in the Buddha's teaching, including a line by line analysis of the mantra. BILINGUAL, Chinese and English. 69-3, $8.50.

VOL. 2. Contains a verse and commentary to explain lines 30 to 90 of the mantra. English/Chinese. 82-0, 200 pgs., $7.50.
VOL. 3. Available Soon.

SONG OF ENLIGHTENMENT - The lyric poem of the state of
the Ch'an sage, by T'ang Dynasty Master Yung Chia.
AVAILABLE SOON.

永嘉大師證道歌詮釋, same as above with commentary
by the Ven. Abbot Hua. CHINESE. 40 pgs., $2.50.

宣化上人偈讚闡釋錄, Verses by the Ven. Abbot Hua.
IN CHINESE. 73 pgs., $5.00.

THE TEN DHARMA REALMS ARE NOT BEYOND A SINGLE THOUGHT.
An eloquent poem on all the realms of being, which is
accompanied by extensive commentarial material and drawings. 72 pgs., 12-X, $4.00.

BIOGRAPHICAL:

    PICTORIAL BIOGRAPHY OF VENERABLE MASTER HSÜ YÜN, Vol.
I. Available Soon.

RECORDS OF THE LIFE OF THE VENERABLE MASTER HSÜAN HUA.
The life and teachings of the Ven. Abbot from his birth-
place in China, to the present time in America.
    VOL. I - covers the Abbot's life in China. 96 pgs.,
    07-3, $5.00. ALSO IN SPANISH, $8.00.
    VOL. II - covers the events of the Abbot's life as he
cultivated and taught his followers in Hong Kong. This
volume contains many photos, poems and stories. 229 pgs.,
10-3, $8.00.

    宣化禪師事蹟/ - same as above, Volumes I and II.
IN CHINESE. 94 pgs., $6.00.

THREE STEPS, ONE BOW - The daily journal of American
Bhikshus Heng Ju and Heng Yo, who in 1973-74 made a re-
ligious pilgrimage from Gold Mountain Monastery in San
Francisco to Marblemount, Washington, bowing every third
step on their way. 160 pgs., 18-9, $5.95.

WORLD PEACE GATHERING - A collection of instructional
talks on Buddhism commemorating the successful comple-
tion of the bowing pilgrimage of Bhikshus Heng Ju and
Heng Yo. 128 pgs., 05-7, $5.00.

WITH ONE HEART BOWING TO THE CITY OF 10,000 BUDDHAS -
The moving journals of American Bhikshus Heng Sure and
Heng Ch'au, who made a "three steps, one bow" pilgrimage from Gold Wheel Temple in Los Angeles to the City
of 10,000 Buddhas, located 110 miles north of San Francisco, from May,1977 to October, 1979.

    VOL. I   - May 6 to June 30, 1977; 180 pgs., 21-9,$6.00.
    VOL. II   - July 1 to October 30, 1977; 322 pgs, 23-5,
                $7.50.
    VOL. III - October 30 to December 16, 1977; 154 pgs.,
                89-8, $6.00.
    VOL. IV   - December 17, 1977 to January 21, 1978; 136
                pgs., 90-1, $5.00.
    VOL. V   - January 22 to February 18, 1978; 127 pgs.,
                91-X, $5.00.
    VOL. VI   - February 19, 1978 to April 2, 1978; 200 pgs.,
                92-8, $6.00.
    VOL. VII - April 3, 1978 to May 24, 1978; 168 pgs.;
                99-5.

Other volumes to appear in sequence, including the
journals from the continuation of "Three Steps One
Bow" within the City of 10,000 Buddhas, still in
progress to date.

修行者的消息 - *NEWS FROM TWO CULTIVATORS* - *LETTERS
OF THREE STEPS, ONE BOW.* The letters from Dharma Masters Heng Sure and Heng Ch'au chronicling the entirety
of their 2 1/2 year journey to reach the City of 10,000
Buddhas. CHINESE only. $7.00.

HENG CH'AU'S JOURNAL - An account of the remarkable experiences and changes undergone by Bhikshu Heng Ch'au
when he first became acquainted with Gold Mountain Monastery. $1.95.

OPEN YOUR EYES, TAKE A LOOK AT THE WORLD - The journals
of Bhikshus Heng Sure and Heng Ch'au and Bhikshuni Heng
Tao, taken during the 1978 Asia-region visit by the Ven.
Abbot Hua together with other members of the Sino-American Buddhist Association. 347 pgs., 32-4, $7.50.

放眼觀世界--亞州弘法記 - the above, in Chinese.
347 pgs., $7.50.

MUSIC, NOVELS, AND BROCHURES:

THREE CART PATRIARCH - A 12" stereo LP recorded by and
for children, based on the Monkey Tales of China.
$7.00 plus $1.00 shipping.

CITY OF 10,000 COLOR BROCHURE - Over 30 color photos of
the center of World Buddhism located in the scenic Men-
docino County near Wonderful Enlightenment Mountain.
24 pgs., $2.00.

CELEBRISI'S JOURNEY - David Round's novel describing
the events in a modern American's quest for enlightenment.
178 pgs., 14-6, $4.00.

VAJRA BODHI SEA 萬佛城 **A monthly journal of ortho-**
dox Buddhism published by the Sino-American Buddhist
Association since 1970. Each issue contains the most
recent translation work of the Buddhist Text Translation
Society, as well as a biography of a great Patriarch of
Buddhism from the ancient past, sketches of the lives
of contemporary monastic and lay followers from around
the world, a Sanskrit lesson, scholarly articles, and
other material. The journal is BILINGUAL in Chinese
and English in an 8 1/2" by 11" format. Single issues
$2.00, one year $22.00, and three years $60.00.

POSTAGE AND HANDLING:

United States: $1.00 for the first book and 40¢ for each
additional book. All publications are sent via special
fourth class. Allow 4 days to 2 weeks for delivery.

International: $1.25 for the first book and 75¢ for each
additional book. All publications are sent via "book
rate." We recommend that for orders of approximately
10 or more, an additional $3.00 per parcel of 100 books
be sent for registration to protect against loss. We
are not responsible for parcels lost in the mail.

*All orders require pre-payment before
they will be processed.*

中文佛書目錄

中美佛教總會法界大學出版

經典部分：

南無阿彌陀佛

南無觀世音菩薩

南無大勢至菩薩

聖作行意村
三其牽其佛
方盡善淨諸
西諸眾自是

④大方廣佛華嚴經十地品淺釋（平裝三冊）　美國萬佛城宣化上人講解。

第一冊（第一歡喜地）（漢英對照）　定價美金七元。

第二冊（第二離垢地。第三發光地。第四餥慧地。第五難勝地）　定價美金五元。

第三冊（第六現前地。第七遠行地。第八不動地。第九善慧地。第十法雲地）定價美金六元。

⑤千手千眼大悲心陀羅尼經（全一冊）　定價美金六元。

⑥般若波羅蜜多心經非台頌解（全一冊）　美國萬佛城宣化上人講解　定價美金五元。

⑦楞嚴咒疏句偈解（漢英對照）（第一冊）　美國萬佛城宣化上人講解　定價美金八元五角。

⑧梵網經講錄（漢英對照）（上冊）　慧僧法師述　定價美金十元。

Dharma Protector Wei To Bodhisattva

Verse of Transference

May the merit and virtue accrued from this work,
Adorn the Buddhas' Pure Lands,
Repaying four kinds of kindness above,
And aiding those suffering in the paths below.

May those who see and hear of this.
All bring forth the resolve for Bodhi,
And when this retribution body is over,
Be born together in ultimate bliss.

$6-50

6.50 -